TEARDROPS IN THE TIDES

THE JOURNEYS OF A "RING FINDER"

JIM WREN

ISBN: 978-1-7320039-0-3

To my wife, Jan

Acknowledgements

There are so many people that I need to say a huge Thank You to for inspiring me to reach goals I didn't think were possible.

Thank you to my rock and my love, my wife Jan who has stood beside me, inspired me, and helped make me who I am today.

Thanks to Chris Turner, who without his dream of making "The Ring Finders" what it is today, I would have never been able to put so many smiles back on faces of complete strangers who thought their treasure was gone forever.

Thanks to Jim Brouwer without your guidance, coaching, encouragement, and help I wouldn't be nearly as successful as I've been to date.

Thanks to Matt Fry, TRF Myrtle Beach SC who has helped me in so many ways. A true friend who's been there when I needed him.

Thanks to my son-in-law Donnie Constransitch, who I got started in this "hobby" and who I can depend on to answer the call when I need his help without hesitation.

A very special Thank you to ALL the individuals that trusted me to help find their lost treasures. With their help on things like times and locations of where they lost their irreplaceable treasures, was enough to enable me to put a smile back on their faces and faith in their hearts.

Disclaimer

Metal detecting can be fun, exciting, and sometimes profitable but at the same time, it can be a demanding, risky, and overall dangerous hobby. Bottom line is you have to use common sense and pay attention to what is doing on around you, or you run a pretty good chance of getting hurt, hopefully not seriously.

If relic hunting is your thing, always make sure you get the landowners permission before detecting. If you are in the woods looking for artifacts and treasures, keep your eyes open for snakes and when you get home, check for ticks. Ensure you have some snacks and water to stay hydrated. Make sure and leave the owner's property better than you found it, fill in your holes and take the trash you found with you.

If you are a beach hunter and plan on getting in the water, you have other concerns. Again, just use common sense, watch the weather, and stay out of the water if there's jellyfish present or rip currents. Be careful how you handle what you dig. In the summertime when the crowds are on the beach, you will probably dig tons of junk. There are plenty of fish hooks, beer cans, bottles, and other things that can cut you. Be careful and pay attention. Just like relic hunting, fill in your holes and take your trash with you.

Lastly, if you are trying to find someone's lost treasure for them be respectful to both them and their property, keep in mind that you must handle their item with care. Remember that what you are looking for is the most precious thing in the world to that person at that very moment.

Contents

Clemson College Class Ring

I got a call from Kaley after she found me in The Ring Finders directory. She told me she had lost her Clemson class ring the night before when she took a 3 a.m. late night stroll on the beach. She informed me she had lost the ring in Myrtle Beach which is The Ring Finders (TRF) member Matt Fry's area of responsibility. I told her I'd call Matt and one of us would be calling her back within the next 10 minutes. I contacted Matt and filled him in on what was going on with the lost ring and its location. He said that he was too busy at work and had a lost ring call to look for that evening. He told me to go ahead and take this lost ring call. I called Kaley back and stated I'd be there in 30 minutes. Matt and I are both members of "The Ring Finders," a global metal detecting service that helps find and return people's lost rings and jewelry. He and I have a great working relationship in regards to respecting each other's areas. We help each other with the hard ring calls or ones that cover large areas. We also fill in for each other when needed.

Before I left home, I did a quick check of the tide tables for the previous night. I determined she lost her ring right at high tide. I thought I'd be there less than an hour.

When I arrived, I met Kaley on the beach. I looked around and noticed that the area was packed with families here on vacation. She gave me the description of the ring and the details of what happened as well as where she was when she lost it. One of her friends, who was with her, had the same ring; so I was able to run a test on my machine and get a visual idea of the lost ring. Kaley also told me she had rented a metal detector and didn't have any luck in finding her ring or anything else for that matter.

I started my grid search, but unfortunately, I was battling a rough incoming tide. At that time, it was getting close to high tide; and I was trying to work around families that were sitting where I needed to search. I told Kaley I'd be back in about an hour and work the outgoing tide. I was hoping that most of the families would be off the beach and gone to dinner when I got back.

When I returned, the tide was outgoing; I think the families had increased though. I was able to work around those in the surf but it wasn't easy. I assumed that if she lost her ring within 30 minutes of high-tide last night, then the ring should be pretty close to the high- tide line and this would be a quick search – not the case!!! As I worked my way down towards the mid-tide line; I think there's no way the ring could be this far down the slope of the beach. Finally at 8:30 p.m. and a good 3 hours of searching the 75 yards of beach that Kaley knew she lost it in, I got a good strong signal. I was a little past the mid-tide line and thought it's unlikely this is the ring, but it's always possible. I dug a scoop full of sand and lightly shook the scoop so I wouldn't damage the ring and saw the gold in the bottom of the scoop. I either had somebody else's ring or hers. I pulled it out of the scoop, and there was no doubt - Booyow, it was hers.

She had told me earlier that she was scheduled to leave sometime that day, so I took a picture and text her "look familiar?" She immediately text me back with "OH MY GOODNESS GRACIOUS!!!" Luckily, she was still in town and finishing up a game of putt-putt golf.

She showed up about 40 minutes later and came running out on the beach smiling from ear to ear. When I handed her ring back to her, she told me that when she lost it at 3 a.m., she called her mom and dad crying. I could relate to that phone call. I got a few big hugs, and many thank yous from Kaley.

I later received these two posts on my blog page. One from Kaley and the other from her father.

Jim,
I don't think I can express the immense gratitude I have for your selfless time spent finding this for me. When my friends and I were out walking on the beach, it didn't even occur to me that my ring could be caught in the waves and disappear from my hand, and in NO way did I think it was possible to find it. To say I was upset is an extreme understatement. After searching for about half an hour with cell phone flashlights, I had to wake up my parents with a very frantic phone call.
I rented a metal detector about seven hours later thinking I would be able to locate the ring somehow myself. When I got it back to the beach, it would not function for more than a matter of seconds, and the frustration had me so disappointed and out of hope that I was about ready to give up. After a quick google search, I can say it was a godsend to find your contact. I'm so grateful that you were willing to make the drive to help me on such short notice. Even when I thought there was no way to find anything amongst all of the people, your determination to keep looking was refreshing and so appreciated. When I received the

picture and your text that you had found it in a matter of hours, I almost cried right in the middle of the putt-putt course. I couldn't believe it!

This ring is very precious to me, in more ways than one. My dad was a Clemson grad, and sharing the tradition of the ring ceremony with him meant the world to me. I also received it alongside my last boyfriend, who was very recently taken from us in a horrific car accident. The ring represents tradition, legacy, and a whole lot of indescribable love... the sentimental value that had me heartbroken to lose. Though my dad tried to convince me that the legacy is what really matters, I knew that this particular ring would be something that I could never replace. Thank you for being a blessing in disguise and not giving up to return to me something that means more to me than you'll ever know. I am forever grateful.

Thank you so much again for all of your patience and perseverance. I wish you the very best and many blessings! Kaley

Jim,

I don't know how to thank you, as mere words cannot express the gratitude we have for what you did. You see, Kaley is my daughter. My one and only! When she called us at 3:00 a.m. and told us her ring was "gone," our hearts sank. We know how much that ring means to her. We purchased the insurance to replace the ring when we bought it. But, to her, it was just "not the same." Knowing that there was NO WAY she would ever find her ring again, I tried to do what any dad would do. I told her it would be okay, "we will get you another one." In my heart, I knew she would never be happy with "another one." Yet we had to do something! She told us she had contacted you and we thought "1 in a trillion chance" that you would find it.

When she forwarded us your text and the picture, we were blown away! This couldn't be. It had to be "lost at sea," "eaten by fish," or "buried forever in the shifting sands." But, YOU did it! You were the one in a trillion. So, from one dad to another, THANK YOU, my friend. THANK YOU, for making my "little girl's" wish a reality.

I know that meeting you and knowing what you did, will always be with her. Your kindness and the generosity of your time means so very much. Thank you again! Have a blessed day!

Introductory – Finding Lost Treasures

Have you ever lost a wedding band, class ring, or a ring that was a family heirloom? I read a statistic that said 4 out of 10 men and 1 in 4 women have lost or misplaced their wedding band at some time in their marriage. Most come up missing doing a leisurely activity and away from home.

In March of 2015, I became a member of "The Ring Finders" which is a global metal detecting service. The service attempts to get lost metallic items, with the use of metal detectors, back to the rightful owner.

Since joining the service, I've had over 70 calls for help in finding a lost item. I've had just about every type of ring search imaginable. I've been from the dry sand on a beach to chest deep in the Atlantic Ocean. I've been in someone's front yard, in a person's vehicle, and in someone's rented condominium. I've heard many different stories on a ring lost and the sentimental importance of it.

Finding lost rings is where "The Ring Finders" can help. This book is about some of my finds and returns and the journey I've taken to get where I am. I've been fortunate in recovering and returning 66 lost treasures, 59 of them were rings, in a little over two years. I've also had the misfortunes of not being able to find items. For what could be one of many reasons I just wasn't able to help find someone's lost treasure.

There are many factors to consider when finding someone's lost gold wedding band in the ocean. It is not just dumb luck. There's a science involved that will be explained later in the book.

Metal Detector Basics

In 2012, my wife, Jan, gave me a metal detector for Christmas. It was a great gift, but I just didn't have the time to fool with it and put it in the garage. About a week after I retired my wife said to me: "You have got to find something to do." I guess I had worn out my welcome of being at home 24/7. I looked at her with that dumb look most husbands have and said: "What?" She reminded me of the metal detector that's been in the garage for more years than she could remember. I had forgotten all about it but thought it might be a pretty good idea.

I had had a little experience with metal detectors, my dad had one when I was a teen, and I remember going out to parks and in the woods with him. He used the detector, and I used the shovel! He did teach me how to use it, and we found a few things. I remember him finding a high school class ring and somehow tracking down the owner and returning it to them, without the internet! I had also gotten my son a detector, and took him out a few times. We found an old ax head that he still has to this day. But like most young teens during those periods in our lives, our attention spans weren't very long. Especially when it came to swinging a machine and digging up junk that had little to no value.

So I broke out my new detecting toy, figured out how to use it, and headed for the beaches in Myrtle Beach, S.C. It was a good machine but only in the dry sand. It just wasn't made for the wet sand or salt water. I started finding a few coins and what many would call junk jewelry, but I was ready for more.

I started doing research, lots of research, on better detectors. My parameters were simple: it had to be in my price range, it had to be easy to learn and use, and it had to be effective. I was reading anything and everything I could find. Like most everything else for any item that has reviews and comments there were as many positives as there were negatives for every machine. Not in every case, but I soon figured out that many of the negative reviews and comments were from individuals who didn't know how to use or set up their machines for optimum performance correctly.

I quickly learned that every machine is excellent on its own, but if the operator doesn't know how to use it or set it up correctly, it's almost useless. Any machine is only as good as the person using it!

Next, I had to figure out what I was going to use the machine to find. Was I only going to detect on the beach? Did I intend to get in the ocean, stay in the wet and dry sand, relic hunt, look for gold nuggets, or something else? I also learned that different settings are necessary on some machines. For instance, if you move from the dry sand to the wet sand and then move again to the water. The bottom line was I had to learn both my limitations and those of the machine to get the optimum performance out of both of us.

I finally decided on the White's Surf PI Dual Field (pulse induction) machine with headphones. I decided I wanted to beach hunt (water and sand) and it met all my parameters. I wanted a machine that I didn't have to worry about it getting wet and ruined. The particular PI I selected can be submerged up to 100 feet deep, not that I'll ever go 100 feet deep in the ocean. I also don't have to make any adjustments going from my backyard to the dry or wet sand or into the surf. Also, the depth on the PI cannot be matched by many machines, which would pay dividends many times over in future recoveries. And best of all, it makes me dig everything; if a target gives me a tone, I dig it. In the process, I do a lot of beach cleaning, removing lots of trash. However, I'm confident I don't leave much, if anything, behind.

The machine I got came with "hard-wired" headphones, meaning they are wired directly into the brains of the detector. Headphones are almost mandatory if you plan on finding things. They're also necessary for some other reasons. First and foremost they save the battery life of the machine. Secondly, they block out all the noises around you, wind, kids asking a million questions, and their parents who ask the same questions their kids just did. Seriously though, they do help block out a lot of outside noise and help you hear the slightest tone change. Lastly, they keep your ears warm in the winter time. You have to have a good pair of headphones.

When I bought the machine, I had no idea I'd be looking for lost treasures on purpose. Now, my thought is if I'm looking for somebody's lost ring or jewelry I want a machine that makes me dig even the faintest signal.

I watched every video I could find on how to use it. I took it out in the backyard and practiced with it. I'd throw pennies, nickels, dimes and quarters in the yard. I'd take my jewelry (rings and watches) and every piece of junk (pull tabs, bottle caps, paper clips, bobby pins and small wire) I could find and practiced finding it. I did the same on the beach, putting the items in sandwich bags and burying them at different depths while adjusting the sensitivity, pulse, and threshold to get the best results for me. I say for me because no two people hear or are comfortable with the same tones, beeps or other sounds that come out of the headsets attached to a metal detector.

Let the Finds Begin

Now that I had my new PI, I was hitting the beaches almost every day. The only problem was I didn't have any idea what I was doing as far as searching the beach. I felt like a wondering fool with the best of intentions but no plan to cover an area thoroughly. I had seen other people on the beach swinging a metal detector so I would watch them and try to gain a few hints. Back to the internet about how, when and where to metal detect. There were some great videos on YouTube and other sites. Little by little I was building confidence and finding more coins and jewelry than before.

I started venturing out into the surf and following the tide changes. I was getting comfortable with how to find the right spots to detect. The more I got out, the more I felt that I knew what I was doing and my finds were starting to increase on a regular basis. I was beginning to find some quality jewelry in the way of gold, platinum, and silver items.

I'm not sure at what point I started to feel a little guilty finding other people's jewelry. Maybe digging up my first man's wedding band that had an inscription inside the band with initials and a date. It just didn't feel right.

I got to the point that when I'd find a ring, I'd go to the nearest hotel or resort and ask the people at the front desk if any of their guests had reported losing a ring. Never had any luck with returning one. There was one front desk person tell me that I could leave the ring with her and she'd attempt to find the owner. Thank you, I appreciated the offer, but it wasn't going to happen. She may have had the best intentions, but I was not going to take the chance.

So with all my concerns, I started searching the internet for sites where people could list their lost or found items. I kept an eye on Craigslist for possible posts on lost rings. I would even post and still do, finds I had made. I have yet to have any luck with making a return to anybody through Craigslist. However, I have been contacted because of my "finding lost jewelry" posts on Craigslist that ended up with recoveries and returns.

In my persistent pursuit to find a solution to my dilemma, I came across "The Ring Finders" website. I read through all the information and many of the stories about other member's recoveries and returns. I learned that this organization was all about helping people that had lost their valued treasures. Finding owners is what I was looking for, and it gave me the opportunity to help people get their lost items back.

The Ring Finders (TRF)

Before I had gotten my first call and recovery, I did a lot of research on and about "The Ring Finders." I read that it is a global metal detecting service with a directory of independent metal detecting specialist who helps people around the world. These members aid in finding lost and most precious and sentimental items, including diamond engagement rings, gold, and platinum wedding bands lost at beaches, parks, lakes, and yards.

I called Chris Turner, Founder, and CEO of The Ring Finders and we talked for a couple of hours. Chris told me how The Ring Finders Directory came to life. His story started in 2009, when a stranger from the United States, who Chris has still not met in person, contacted him after seeing his metal detecting service in Vancouver, Canada, called "Finders." The gentleman introduced himself over the phone and mentioned that he'd been following Chris' website for years. He went on to say how wonderful it was that Chris found a way to use his metal detector to help people recover their lost jewelry, and how happy it was making people. The gentleman asked Chris if he ever thought of creating a global directory so that he could share his ideas with other metal detectorists and thereby, help more people. Chris told him, "Yes, but a new website wasn't in his budget at the time." The gentleman's response was, "You create it, and I'll pay for it." And he did!

Chris said that in late October of 2009 The Ring Finders Directory was incorporated. With very little advertising, it has steadily grown during the past eight years. Collectively, The Ring Finders members are responsible for finding and returning more than 4100 lost rings with a combined value exceeding $6.8 million. These figures were as of January 2018.

Expanding this service worldwide has enabled many people the opportunity to have their lost jewelry found and returned. Before this, the possibility did not exist at this level. The directory includes members in all fifty states in the US (total of 680) and 26 countries. Ninety-seven percent of the members work on a reward basis. Most members have a call out fee if the item isn't found to cover the cost of gas.

Chris told me about some of his fabulous recoveries and returns and the stories that went with them. I also read many of the other member's stories thinking this is a very dedicated bunch of men and woman that are very passionate about what they are doing. I was hooked and joined The Ring Finders in 2015 and have not looked back. My areas of responsibility include North Myrtle Beach, S.C., as well as Shallotte, N.C., which is located in the Southeast Corner of North Carolina and includes Sunset Beach, Ocean Isle Beach, Holden Beach and Oak Island Beach.

Losing Keepsake Jewelry

Some thirty years ago my mother had bought my son a pretty expensive ring that he lost within the first week of receiving it as a gift. So many thoughts went through my mind when he lost it. My mother didn't have the money to buy it in the first place, how can we replace it, and is it possible to find it. He lost it in a camper so it couldn't be too hard to find, but boy was I wrong. I remember tearing that camper up trying to find the ring with no luck. I've never forgotten the pain and guilt of losing that ring forever.

I learned from Chris Turner, other members of The Ring Finders, and in my own experience that every ring or piece of jewelry has a story attached to it. It makes no difference whether the item cost a few dollars or tens of thousands of dollars, it still has a story. The story may have started the day before when a young couple got married and placed the rings on each other's fingers. It could have started generations ago when a parent passed their keepsake down to a child who then passed it down to their child. It could represent an individual's personal accomplishment like high school or college graduation, military service, or a memory of something important to them. Losing a sentimental item is devastating in itself, but when it's gone the story that goes with it comes to a stop.

The goal of The Ring Finders is to recover a lost item and get it back where it belongs so the story can continue. Like I mentioned earlier in the book, members of The Ring Finders have been able to keep over 4100 stories going.

With the recoveries and returns I've made, no two stories are the same. I've had men and women overwhelmed and cried on my shoulder, and I've shed some tears as well. I've had hugs that are so sincere and tight that it almost hurt. I've been called an angel, guardian angel, man of miracles, and a savior. Experiences like those are indescribable about how it makes you feel inside. Making returns and getting those responses are what it's all about for The Ring Finders. It just couldn't get any better than seeing the tears and smiles you get when you hand something thought to be gone forever back to its rightful owner.

Wind, Waves, Tides, and Sand

Now is a good time to talk about all the contributing factors that can either help or hinder finding someone's ring on the beach or in the ocean. These are the effects of the wind, waves, tides, and sand. I can't speak about any other beaches than the ones I hunt in North and South Carolina. There's even a difference in tides between North and South Carolina beaches as far as the distances and time of day between high and low tides.

I'm not going to talk about how to read the ocean and beach to find the low spots, washouts, real and fake runnels, holes and other clues the beach can tell you. One of the best resources for that information that I know of is in a book written by a good friend, Jim Brouwer called *"**Gold Beneath The Waves, Treasure Hunting The Surf and Sand.**"* Jim explains in great detail, with pictures, on how to read a beach to get the best results. It's a fantastic book and has taught me a lot.

When someone loses a ring at the beach, if it's a heavyweight metal like gold, platinum, tungsten, etc. it's going to sink into the sand immediately. A person can be in waist-deep water at high tide, and the ring will come off their finger and pretty much go straight down and settle into the sand. By the time the tide has turned and reached the low tide line the lost ring is now around the mid-tide line, and much easier to find. Heavy metals won't be too affected by the waves and currents like the lighter metals, mainly silver or small gold rings. Lighter rings will move a little more but still should be in the same general area.

While a ring is sitting in the sand, the waves and current are moving sand back and forth covering and uncovering it. Then the winds and tides help move more sand back and forth up and down the beach covering and uncovering the ring. Big storms, tropical depressions, and hurricanes can play havoc on beaches, either blowing tons of sand onto the beach or pulling tons of sand off the beach. It all depends on the proximity of the storm to the beach.

If someone calls me on a lost ring within a few hours of losing it, it gives me a much better chance of finding the ring than if they call me two, three, or more days later. If the lost ring is in the dry sand, once again the sooner I get called, the better. There's a much better chance of finding it than if it's lost in the ocean. Here in the Myrtle Beach area, we have a lot of local people that metal detect almost daily. There's also a hoard of tourist who comes on vacation with metal detectors in hand. The local folks are very good at what they do and have the equipment to find the hard targets. Some of the tourists are just as equipped and as good as the locals, and some aren't. But as the old saying goes, "even a blind squirrel can find a nut once in a while" holds true here. There is always a chance somebody else is going to find the lost item before the owner can make arrangements for somebody to look for them.

Now, when I get called or emailed asking for help in finding a ring I ask a lot more questions than I did in the beginning. I want to know where they lost it, as in which resort or hotel, what day and time it was, was the person in dry sand, wet sand, or in the ocean? If they were in the water how deep were they (ankle, knee, waist, or chest deep)? It seems like a lot of questions, but the answers narrow the search which gives me a much better chance of finding their lost item.

One of the first things I'll do is check the tide tables and find out where the tides were on the day and time of the loss. Did it happen at the high, mid, or low tide, was the tide going out or coming in. There have been times I've had to wait 12-24 hours before I could look for the ring because of the tide changes or the time of the next low tide. You can pretty much rest assured that I'm not going out at 2, 3, or 4 a.m. if that's the next low tide. I'll wait until the next afternoon tide change; it's safer all the way around. I'm also not going out in a thunderstorm when there's lightning in the area. Being out there then is not a good idea when I'm walking along the water holding a machine that has a metal shaft on it. Rain is not a problem but no lightning!

What I've come to realize, is that for the most part, ladies lose their rings in the dry sand to the high tide line. They're the ones that put the suntan lotion on themselves, the kids and the husband. They take their rings off and put them on their lap, or they throw them in their bag and miss. They also walk down to the high tide line to rinse their hands off or wash the sand off their legs and feet, and their rings slide off their fingers. Men, on the other hand, lose their rings lower on the beach or in the ocean. They're playing with the kids, body surfing, throwing a ball or just standing in the pounding waves. The younger married guys usually lose their rings in the deeper water. It seems they like to see how deep in the ocean they can get before they drown. If someone gets out past the sandbar and loses their ring, it's pretty much gone. With the waves and current, it's like a washing machine out there. Out that far, rings quickly drop through the sand, never to be seen again.

Search Patterns

There's another vital factor to consider when searching for someone's ring, how to do the actual search, so you're methodical. It can be devastating to someone who just lost their wedding band or other significant items. Then they tell you they think it's in an area about half the size of a football field or more. That's a lot of beach to cover, and I've had many of those calls, they're time-consuming, and they're not fun. My goal is to find and return the ring, nothing more and nothing less, so I'm not a bit hesitant to call for help. There are three individuals (Jim Brouwer, Matt Fry - TRF Myrtle Beach, and my son-in-law, Donnie Constransitch), that I know I can count on no matter what. I know they're as dedicated and determined as I am and I've asked for their help on some occasions. Whether I do the search by myself or get help, to completely cover the area, there has to be a pattern.

There's a couple of search patterns I use, one is what I call a square line grid, and the other is a circular grid. I prefer the square line search. It's easy to follow and ensures complete coverage of the area. You draw a box or rectangle in the sand with your scoop around the search area. Then you start your search in one corner, walk to the far corner, take a step or two to the right or left and then walk back in the opposite direction to the box outline. Drag you scoop in the sand behind you so you can keep track of your grid lines and you don't miss an area. Make sure your detector swings or sweeps overlap each other. Something I've got in the habit of is extending my search zone an extra 10 to 15 feet outside the area the owner told me, it usually saves me time and effort in the long run.

Even when you're waist deep in the Atlantic one needs to be methodical and try to grid. When waves are pushing you around it adds another level of difficulty. If I am gridding parallel to the low tide line, I try to use my depth and distance from that line as a gauge to cover the area. Gridding from shallow to deep water is somewhat easier because you can use landmarks to keep a straight line. I want to know that I have had my coil over every inch of the area to find the lost ring.

SQUARE LINE GRID SEARCH

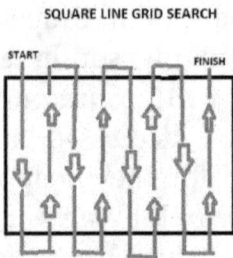

Here are three examples of searching an area. As illustrated, my square line and circular grid searches are far more effective in covering an area. With the non-grid search, it's very haphazard. With this method, there's a good chance that you'll over search one area while completely missing another.

Circular Grid

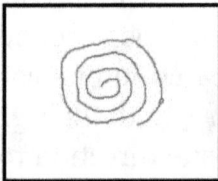

NON-GRID SEARCH

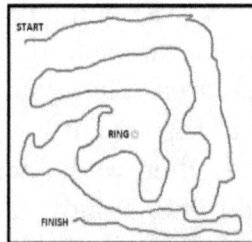

Not all Fun, Sun, or Finds

Throughout my time as a member of The Ring Finders, I've been pretty fortunate, lucky, blessed, or just in the right place at the right time. You can call it what you want. If you think about it, finding people's lost rings or other valuable and sentimental small pieces of jewelry compares to the proverbial "finding a needle in a haystack." There are three major differences though. First, in this case, the "needle" I'm looking for is somewhere between the size of a dime to a quarter but not as thick. Secondly, the "haystack" I'm looking for it in, is usually either tons of sand spread over a large area or its millions of gallons of water that pushes you around like you're a leaf in a windstorm. Lastly, the "needles" I'm trying to find cost hundreds to tens of thousands of dollars.

When I get a call, I take it very personally in that I know someone is hurting deep inside. The stricken owner can always buy a new replacement, after all, it's just a materialistic piece of metal, but it will never have the same feel, meaning, or story. It's vital to do everything possible to find their lost treasure. Imagine if you or your spouse lost a wedding ring, would either of you be happy with a replacement? My wife or I wouldn't! Like I said earlier, every lost ring has a story and when it's lost the story stops. I've had some I just couldn't find, and it breaks my heart. I'm a very dedicated and persistent person by nature. I don't give up unless I'm 100% confident that I've covered every inch of the area and felt there's just nothing else I can do. I've gone back to areas over and over again, researched the area, used different machines, and even called somebody to help me search. Every once in a while, going back numerous times or going with somebody else has paid off but not too often. I just hate walking away from somebody's lost treasure. But it happens, unfortunately.

I feel there are three reasons why I couldn't find a ring or something else for somebody. The first reason I couldn't find an item is that I don't think the owner had me in the right spot or the spot was inaccessible, because of the depth of water. Secondly, and probably the main reason is the beach conditions. I can't overemphasize this, the longer the "needle" sits in the sand, the more it gets buried until it's so covered up, it's just too far down for a metal detector to find. Lastly, someone else stumbled across it before I got there, which happens a lot more than you'd think. There's a lot of people metal detecting at the beach on a daily basis. I know they find things because I've seen the holes they leave in the sand. There's one fellow that comes down here from the north and is here three to four months during the winter every year. He knows what he's doing, has plenty of spare time, and has a top of the line metal detector, so he finds a lot of lost items. Not that long ago, he had recovered sixteen rings in a two week period. The finds weren't all wedding bands, but they were still someone's treasure.

I've included a few of my unsuccessful searches in each chapter, to show that not everything is perfect when looking for someone's treasure. Sometimes the conditions, delays in calling, or just not being in the right spot can cause a ring or other item not to be found. When something sentimental is gone forever, it's hard for everybody involved.

Quickies

It's not often that someone calls immediately after losing their ring or other valuable treasure. Reason being, most people don't know a service like The Ring Finders exists. What I've found out in my short term as a ring finder is that it's usually the younger generation that finds me within a couple of hours. Almost everyone has a cell phone now, and they take them everywhere, including the beach. I know, because I've found phones destroyed due to being buried in the sand and salt water. As I was saying, the younger folks know how to use their phones and find everything they need to know about any subject with the help of the internet. Those that don't think to try their phones to find somebody to help them, wait until they get back home. That delay could mean the difference between finding and returning an item or never seeing it again.

Another major help in finding and returning an item is to know where you lost it. Metal detecting is indeed a game of inches, so if you drop something, stop and look around for landmarks. Pace off the distance to stationary landmarks like a signpost, fence post, rental chair stands, or stairways. The more details you can provide the better the odds of getting your item back where it belongs. Another thing people have done to help find their object is google earth and pin the area. It works!

The stories in this chapter are innocently referred to as "quickies" because they were all very quick and easy recoveries. Whether it was because someone contacted me within a couple of hours after the loss, the owner knew where they lost their item or both; it made my search a lot simpler. Most of the returns here took me longer to get to the location than it did to find the item. I consider finding a lost object under an hour as quick.

First Call, Recovery, and Return

While out shopping with my wife, daughter, and granddaughter I received a call from a young lady who was very upset. She had lost her wedding band. She said she was digging in the sand with her son and thought she should take both her engagement ring and wedding band off. She told me she put them in a bag next to her towel and when she went to retrieve them only the engagement ring was in the bag. I got the name of the hotel in North Myrtle Beach, S.C. where they were staying, and told her I could be there in about an hour to an hour and a half.

We finished up our shopping, and I ran my daughter and granddaughter home. I then drove my wife home and picked up my detecting gear. Then off to the beach, I went.

Ok, this was my first ring call, my moment of truth, was I ready to find somebody's treasure? Someone was relying on me to locate and return their lost treasure! I was full of all kinds of emotions, and I won't lie to you – I was nervous! It's hard for me to compare this to anything else I've gone through in life. I was just praying to GOD that I had the skills and knowledge to complete the task successfully. So here we go.

When I arrived at the beach, I called her, and she quickly met me at the beach entrance. We walked down to their spot in the sand where I met her husband and family. Her husband had already marked a 15 X 20 foot square in the sand around the area they had been sitting.

Right away I realized two things; one is that I had to turn into an investigator to get all the details about the item, the suspected area of loss, and the circumstances that caused the object to get lost. Were they throwing or catching a ball, had they put the item on a towel and then shook it, slinging the ring(s) into the sand, or did they put the article in a cup holder on a beach chair and then moved the chair. All these things have happened and can affect the search area. Secondly, I had to set some ground rules or a verbal contract, if you will, to protect myself. Naturally, anything else I might find while looking for their item is mine, and I'm not responsible if the item is damaged, like a missing stone. Luckily, I haven't recovered a damaged object. I have found another man's wedding band in the process of looking for and retrieving a different man's wedding ring.

So I asked the young lady to describe her ring, what exactly happened, and the general area it was dropped. Even though I knew the story and that her husband had the area marked off, a second version never hurts. Sometimes an individual or family member remembers something new or a little different, after the initial shock of losing the item, which helps in the search. She told me her ring was a 14K White Gold wedding band that matched the engagement ring she had on her finger. Perfect, I asked her if I could test her engagement ring to make sure my detector could detect it and I could hear it. Everything was working fine, so the only thing left was to find her treasure. I set a north/south grid, parallel to the tide line, and started searching. The first grid line produced a pull tab, the second grid line produced a house or room key, and when I looked at her, I could see her hope in finding her ring was fading. There was nothing on the third grid line. As I turned to do the fourth line I got a good signal with my PI and dug a shallow scoop of sand. I double checked the hole to ensure I had the target in the scoop. After lightly shaking out the sand I couldn't see anything with the seagrass in the scoop, so I gently shook the scoop one more time – bingo!!! There was her size five wedding band. I reached in the scoop, looked at her, gave her a little smile and a wink and nodded my head for her to come over to me. She covered her mouth with both hands, and I'm pretty sure tears started rolling out of both of our eyes. I held my closed fist out and dropped the ring in her outstretched hands and then got one of the biggest hugs I've ever had. I got extra hugs and handshakes from her husband, dad and a couple of other relatives. It was amazing and something I'll never forget. Total search time was less than 5 minutes. Her dad called me her guardian angel. My first recovery was a complete success; whew was I happy!!

Luckily, my first recovery and return was an easy, and quick one that I will never forget. It was a great confidence builder, but it also taught me a lot of valuable lessons I still use today.

Quickies

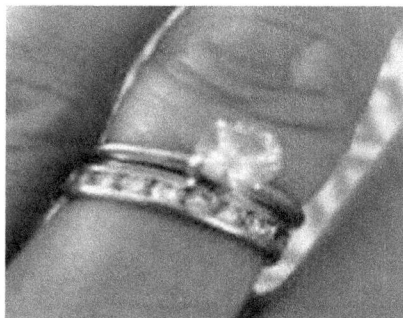

Father and Son Playing Catch

Jimmy called me about mid-morning asking if I could help find his lost wedding band. His wife Crystal had googled "Lost Ring Ocean Isle" and up popped The Ring Finders website as well as one of my blogs. Jimmy told me he and his family were on vacation from Va. and were enjoying a day on the beach. He went on to say that he lost the ring the day before, in about thigh-high water. He continued, saying he was throwing a ball back and forth with his son Caleb when the ring came off. We agreed to meet in about an hour, and I was on my way.

When I got to the beach, Jimmy, Crystal, and Caleb met me at the beach access. On the way out to the beach I got a few more details, and then Caleb walked us out to the area his dad was at when the ring slipped off his finger. The big question was whether Jimmy was right or left handed and did the ring slip off his finger or get slung off as he threw the ball. Luckily, he's right-handed, so it made for an easier search.

Jimmy put me in the area he thought he lost it in, Caleb thought it might be a little further south. I split the difference and started a north/south grid line at the low tide line first. From the details I got from both Jimmy and Caleb, I was confident the ring hadn't worked its way to the low tide line, but you never know. With an incoming tide, I didn't want to miss the opportunity of searching that area before it was under water. After clearing that area, I then moved up the beach to the high tide line. People were starting to show up and set up their umbrella's and towels. I didn't want to miss searching that area and wanted to do it before it got too crowded to detect. After a few search lines to clear the high tide line, I moved to an east/west grid search, which was perpendicular to the ocean. I extended the search area to cover both Jimmy's and Caleb's areas. After about 5 or 6 search lines I got a reliable signal, pretty sure I had found the ring. I dug out a scoop of sand and dumped it out on the beach, and there was a man's gold wedding band. I picked it up, cleaned the sand off and saw an inscription on the inside. Jimmy's son was close and saw me hold up my hand and wave towards Jimmy. Caleb came running over, checked the inscription on the inside of the ring and confirmed it was his dad's ring. I had Jimmy's ring!

Jimmy was trying to keep himself busy further down the beach because he was afraid I wouldn't find it and didn't want to watch me. He and Crystal made their way over and were extremely happy. I handed his ring back to him, and the 24-year story it held will continue. Hugs and handshakes all around.

I received the following from Crystal on my post

Thank you again for finding the lost wedding band! While needing your services was unfortunate, we were blessed to meet you and thank you for what you do.

Lost While Enjoying the Evening

Mark sent me a late evening email saying he was on Pawley's Island S.C. vacationing with his wife, Colleen, and family from Pa. He asked if I could help find his wedding band. I responded saying I'd be glad to help and I could be there the next day at 2 p.m. He said he had lost it in the dry sand behind their home, so I wasn't too concerned it'd get buried, or someone else would find it.

I arrived at the address Mark sent me, and he was waiting in his driveway. He walked me out to the beach and showed me the small area he believed his ring was lost the night before. Mark and his family had been sitting on the beach enjoying the evening. He continued by saying that he had taken his ring off and put it in the cup holder on his beach chair. A couple of hours later after returning to their beach house, he realized he didn't have his ring and had forgotten it in the chair that was now on the back deck.

Before I started my grid search, I wanted to double check the chair he used and the path he'd taken from the beach to the deck where he ended up putting the chairs for the night. No luck with finding his ring in either the chair or the path he would have taken.

I moved out on the beach in the area they sat and started a grid search. No sooner did I start, and I started having problems with my PI giving off a loud constant steady tone, which was probably a bad battery. Usually, I have a consistent whisper tone that erupts when I pass over a metal object. Luckily, I had brought my Garrett AT Pro and saved myself a 45-minute drive back home. The small area wasn't yielding a ring after about 30 minutes. Mark suggested he might have been a little farther south than he thought. I expanded my grid search out even farther than my usual 10 to 15 feet, and I hit a good signal. I dug a shallow scoop of sand, and I HAD IT. I kept the ring in the scoop as I extended it out to Mark to retrieve his treasure. He and Colleen were excited and thankful to have his ring back on his finger where it belonged. A couple of handshakes and I was on my way home with another happy return completed.

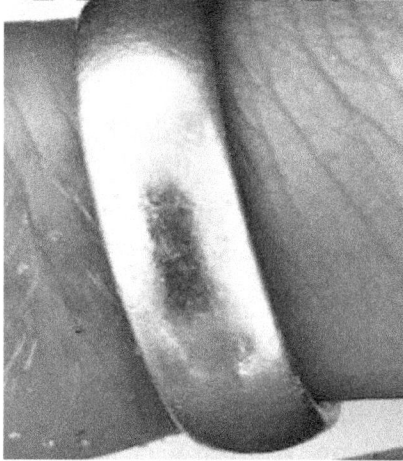

Weekend Trip

On a Sunday night, I got an email from Daniel telling me he had lost his wedding band on the beach at Oak Island, N.C. the previous Friday. In the email, he asked if I would be willing to drive to Oak Island and see if I could find it. I responded saying yes that it'd be no problem and then asked the same questions – where on the beach, the time he lost it and the ring description.

The next morning Daniel had followed up with his responses as well as calling me. He knew exactly where he had been, what time it was and even down to the number of paces it was from the soft sand into the high tide line. Looking at the current tide tables, I saw I had about 4 hours before high tide, so I headed out for the hour drive up to Oak Island. Once I got to the beach, I followed his directions, and he couldn't have been more exact on where it was. On my third grid line, in ankle deep water I got the signal. Two scoops and I had his wedding band in my hand. I took a picture of his ring and sent it to him with a text saying "Bingo."

While I'm standing on the beach waiting for his response, I noticed two ladies walking towards me. They walked up to me and introduced themselves as Daniel's mother and his Aunt and informed me that Daniel had called them that morning letting them know I was going to be looking for it. They thought they'd come down and watch. I told them I had already found it and had just sent Daniel a picture and text and was waiting for his response. Neither one of them could believe I had found it in the first place let alone so quickly. Both ladies were surprised and excited for Daniel. Shortly after I met his mother and aunt, Daniel called and was very happy about his ring. So I didn't have to mail his ring, he told me to go ahead and give it to his mother. A quick search with another great ending to a lost ring story.

Missed the X's

I got an email from Kim asking if I could help find her husband Trevor's lost wedding band on Ocean Isle Beach, N.C. I responded saying that there shouldn't be a problem and we agreed to meet at low tide, about 7:30 p.m. During the 30-minute drive, I noticed a nasty storm brewing and moving my way quickly.

I met Kim, and as we're walking towards the beach access, she told me what happened. She said her husband had lost his ring the day before while wave surfing with the kids. They had been out later that same afternoon and searched with no luck. Her husband didn't want to waste any more vacation time looking for his ring: that he thought was gone for good, so they gave up the search.

She said she had (discreetly) looked on the internet and found me through The Ring Finders directory and decided to contact me for help.

We walked out on the beach to an area in the wet sand marked on all four corners with a big X drawn in the sand. I'm watching the storm move closer, with big lightning strikes off in the distance. I started my grid search. I wasn't finding anything between the X's so she told me that the ring could be a little outside of the Xs. I moved a little to the north side of the Xs she had previously marked and started the grid.

This search was one of the rare times I hadn't expanded the grid search in the first place, which probably cost me some extra time. On my third row, I hit a good solid 59-60 on my AT Pro machine which is what a 14k gold ring would show up as. It took me three scoops to get the ring out of the hole, which was pretty covered up with sand considering it had only been there 24 hours. I dumped the sand on the beach, spread it out with my foot and saw a small glimmer of gold. I reached down and picked it up, blew the sand off the ring and turned around to give it to Kim. She was overwhelmed with joy, and a few tears were shed, which gets me every time!

I got a huge hug from Kim just as her husband and three kids were walking from the beach access onto the beach. I think she had text him that we found his ring while I was filling up the hole. He was happy as well.

I received the following in my post from Kim.

True story. Jim was WONDERFUL!! Do not hesitate to call him. I only wish I had called him the day it happened so we didn't spend a whole day of our vacation looking for the ring!

Diamonds in the Sand

Jamil called me a little after 11 a.m. on a bright and sunning day. He told me his wife had lost her wedding and engagement rings in the sand and asked if I could help find them. He said they were in the soft sand so this was going to be a quick search. The only problem was it was in Myrtle Beach, so I needed to call Matt Fry, the TRF for Myrtle Beach. Matt told me to go ahead and take the call. I called Jamil back and let him know I was on my way.

I met Jamil and his wife, Khatira, on the beach with their two small children. Khatira told me she had taken her rings off and placed them on her lap and forgot about them. A few minutes later she stood up, and her rings went flying into the soft sand. She and Jamil looked for them by shifting the sand back and forth seeing if they could spot them. After hunting in desperation with no success, I believe, they looked up lost rings in Myrtle Beach on their iPhone. They found me through one of my blogs on finding lost rings.

Khatira showed me the area where she was sitting, and I started a grid search. I searched the area for about 5 minutes and didn't have any signals. Right behind their spot, was a beach umbrella and chairs that were locked together. I asked Jamil if he could get the lifeguard so we could unlock and move the umbrella and chairs. It only took a few minutes for the lifeguard to show up. I explained to him that I was on a ring search and he gladly unlocked and moved the umbrella and chairs. Once those were out of the way, I got my first tone.

I took a scoop of sand and dumped in on the beach. I ran my detector coil over the pile to make sure

I had the target. I then spread the sand out with my foot and saw her engagement ring. I handed her the engagement ring and got a smile! One more ring to find. A few more passes with the detector and I got the second tone and scooped up her wedding band. When I handed it to her, I got a big smile, and many thank yous. Another happy and relieved couple with another saved vacation. Total search and recovery time was about 10 minutes.

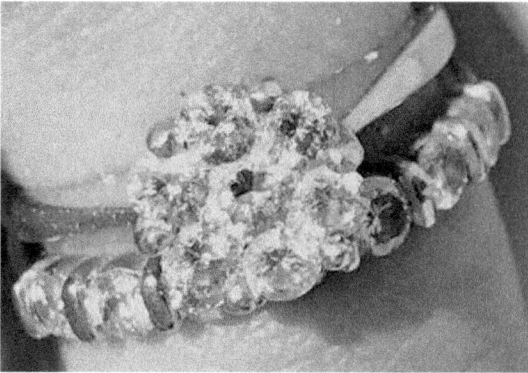

Lost by a Little Angel

I got a call at about 11:15 a.m. from David saying his wife, Rose, had lost her Wedding and Engagement Ring set. He said they were dropped in the dry sand and wanted to know if I could help find them. I got his location and told him it should be a quick, and easy search and I'd be there in 15-20 minutes.

I called David when I got close, and he met me in the parking lot. On the way out to the beach, he explained that he and his wife suspected their little daughter of losing the rings. They believed that she might have picked the rings up out of the cup holder in the beach chair and then dropped them in the sand. Once we got on the beach, I met Rose and the little culprit, who looked so innocent.

It was another beautiful sunny day, and the beach was starting to get crowded with the summer tourist. Rose described the rings and showed me the area she suspected they were. Luckily, the spot hadn't been taken over by other beachgoers yet. I made a line in the dry sand with my scoop to outline my grid area. The area only measured roughly 10 X 15 feet, so this wouldn't be hard. To help me out, David and Rose cleared the beach umbrella, beach chairs, and other items from inside the search area. I started my grid search, and on the third pass I had a clear tone, dug a scoop of sand, and had her ring set.

I turned around to Rose and asked her again what the ring set looked like, but she was way ahead of me. She knew I had found the rings because she heard the ring rattle in the scoop as I lightly shook out the sand. I held the scoop out and let her pull her treasure out. Another ring recovery and return with big smiles all the way around. Total search and recovery time was under 2 minutes.

Long Way from Home

Laura sent me a text message about 8:30 p.m. on May 14th after finding me through The Ring Finders website directory. She asked if I could help find her husband's wedding band that he lost in the surf. I called her right back and got the location and description of the ring and was on my way.

Laura and her husband Chris were staying in one of the campgrounds in Surfside S.C. I got there in about an hour and called Laura so she could meet me near the front gate. Without proof that you are staying on the campgrounds, you are not going to get past the gate guard. We met in the parking lot and had to go inside the main building to get me a guest pass. I think there's a 10 dollar charge for the pass, no matter how long you're visiting. I had to leave my car in the main building's parking lot and hop in the golf cart Chris was driving.

Chris drove us to the beach and showed me the area where the ring had come off his finger. They told me this was the first day of their big family vacation and were here from Anchorage, Alaska. Chris told me this was a custom made ring and very special to him. He said he had lost the ring roughly one and half hours after high tide. By the time I got there to search it was low tide, so I was in luck of finding it without having to get in the water and get wet.

I started a north/south grid search at about the mid-tide line and worked towards the surf. The search area wasn't all that big, and I wanted to eliminate the lower part of the beach before the tide change, and I'd be fighting an incoming tide. I searched for about thirty minutes, confident that I had thoroughly covered the area without having any luck.

I then started working an east/west grid line from the mid tide line towards the dry sand. After about fifteen minutes and three grid lines, I had a shallow signal. I dug one scoop of sand out of the hole, shook the sand out and there it was. I reached in and plucked it out and had his ring in my hand. I cleaned it off, put it back in my scoop and walked back over to where Chris and Laura were standing. I asked him to describe his ring one more time. As he's telling me about his ring, I turned my headlamp on, pointed it in the scoop and asked: "does it look like this." Bam, I think all three of us dropped a tear or two.

This search turned out to be an easy one, a little time consuming but I wanted to make sure I took my time and found his ring on my first try. I'm sure they enjoyed the rest of their vacation. Chris and Laura ran me back to the car, and I was on my way back home with another wedding band saved.

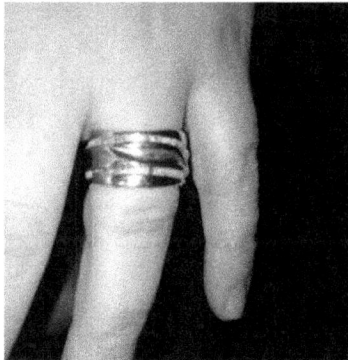

Last Day of the Vacation

Joe sent me an email then followed it up with a phone call. He said he was here on vacation with his family, from Ohio. He told me he had lost his Tungsten wedding band about an hour ago in the surf and was wondering if I could help find it. I got the location of the resort and checked the tide tables. If he lost it an hour ago, we should be in pretty good shape for finding it. There was an outgoing tide so his ring ought to be right at mid-tide. I told him I'd be there in 20 minutes. This resort was gated so I needed him to alert the guard that I'd be coming.

When I got there, the gate guard waved me through and told me to park right up front next to the pool area. Joe's dad, Russell, was waiting at the guard shack to escort me to the beach area, so he jumped in the car and rode with me to park. I grabbed my gear out of the car and Russell, and I headed through the swimming pool area out onto the beach.

Shortly after Russell and I got to the approximate area, I started a grid search. Joe showed up and moved me a little and put me just about dead on the spot. On my second pass, I got the signal, but it took me three scoops to remove the target out of the hole. I was wondering if I had Joe's ring or a deep bottle cap. Having just lost his ring, this was a lot deeper than I thought it should be. Then again, Tungsten is a heavy metal so it'll sink fast. I flattened out the sand I had scooped with my foot and saw the outline of a ring. I brushed it off, and it was the right one!!!

Joe and Russell were both amazed we found it. Joe's wife, Maria, and his mother were looking down from the resort balcony as Joe waved that we had it. This return was another must find because they were heading home the next day. Now they've got a bigger story to tell about their vacation.

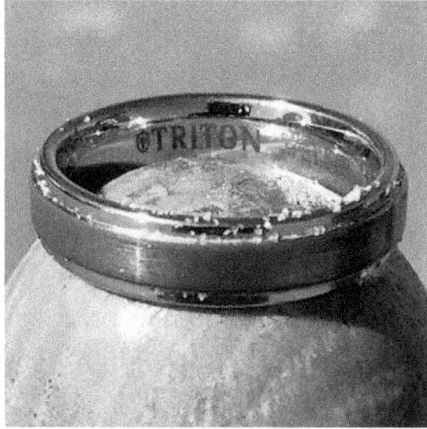

12th Fairway

Besides hazards on the beach and ocean, there are hazards in the grass as well. I got a call from a young man saying he was in Myrtle Beach about three weeks ago, playing golf. He and his buddies had played a round of golf at one of the better clubs. He said he had put his college class ring in one of the pockets on his golf bag before he started playing. He had a good game going, and everything was fine. He remembers being on the 12th fairway when he and his friends decided to light up cigars and smoke them as they finished out the round. He told me the cigars were in the same pocket where he had put his class ring. When they finished up the round of golf, he went for his ring, and it was gone.

He was confident the ring came out with the cigars and knew where on the fairway he was. He gave me a description of the fairway. He included how close he had his golf cart to the bunker that was along the side of the fairway. He said he had reported the loss to the Pro shop but hadn't heard anything and was wondering if I could look. I agreed thinking someone had to have found and kept it after all this time.

I stopped by the Pro shop and told them what the situation was. The guy at the counter remembered somebody losing his class ring, in fact, he showed me the card with the phone number that was left. I asked if I could go to the 12th fairway and look for it. I also ensured him I was not going to dig up the fairway. He told me to go ahead but be careful and courteous to the golfers on that hole. Being a golfer myself, I knew what he was saying, getting hit with a golf ball hurts like hell!

Thankfully, the fairway was along one of the roadways in the community, so I didn't have to walk or try to get a cart. As I pulled off the road by the hole, there was a twosome just finishing up.

I made my way around the hole, and up the fairway. I kept my eyes on the tee box as I started searching in and around the bunker. I noticed another twosome in the tee box, so I backed off the fairway and got out of the way. Once they got to the green, I started a grid from one side of the fairway to the other. Probably about the 6th or 7th grid line, right in the middle of the fairway, I got the sound of gold in the headset. I moved the grass a little and saw a piece of the ring, Uh-Oh!!! I picked it up, and there was enough of it left that I could make out the name of the College, and I had a match. What happened was that over the course of 3 weeks the grass had been mowed, probably numerous times. I'm sure the ring was sitting up just high enough in the grass that the lawnmower caught it and chopped it into pieces. Gold is a soft metal, and the blades on a lawn mower will tear it up. I searched around for some more of the ring but didn't find any other pieces. I'd say that the other pieces were slung in all directions two or three times, at least. I thought I was pretty lucky to find any part of the ring. I stopped back by the clubhouse and told them they didn't need to keep his card any longer and showed them the piece of the ring. I called the guy back and told him what happened and sent him a clear picture with the college name visible. He was thankful I'd found what I did and said that at least he had closure about the ring. He thanked me, and we hung up.

Followed the Ball

After having two unsuccessful ring hunts on the same day, I was ready for a change of luck. The first call that morning was a lady that had lost her ring after she said she had put it in one of the pockets on her golf bag. She was sure she put the ring in the bag at the bag drop before the 1st hole. When she finished the 18th hole, it wasn't there. She asked me if I'd look at the bag drop to the 1st tee box, I did, and nothing. Then she asked if I'd search around the 18th where she started collecting her items out of the bag, again I did, and still nothing. Her husband and I think she probably dropped it around the bag drop and someone picked it up and kept it.

The second call was for a man's wedding ring that was "possibly" lost in the wet sand two days before. It was one of those calls where they know they lost their ring but not sure where. It could be in one of many places they visited between the time they last saw it on his finger, and then realized it was gone hours later. Unfortunately, I wasn't able to find that one either.

As I was leaving the beach after the second hunt, I checked my email and saw the mail from Philip. His email said he had lost his Tungsten Wedding band in about 2 feet of water earlier in the afternoon. He finished his email asking if I could help find it. I emailed him back saying I was on my way. I also included my cell phone number and asked him to call me.

About five minutes from his location, he called, and we agreed to meet on the beach. As I'm walking out on the beach, I see a young man walking along the surf line looking a little desperate. We greeted, and I had him explain what had happened. He said he and his friends had been throwing a ball around when his ring flew off his finger. Losing a ring while throwing a ball is never a good thing, it's hard to determine the trajectory, especially in the ocean. Luckily, he lost it on an outgoing tide so what was 2 feet deep when it happened is now probably about ankle deep. On the other hand, it could be a lot deeper depending on what direction and how hard he was throwing the ball. This search could be very challenging but it was a beautiful evening with small waves, the water was warm, and I had about three and a half hours before it got dark.

I asked him if he had anything planned because this may take a little while. He said he and his buddies had planned on going to dinner someplace. I told him that he didn't need to stick around and suggested he go ahead and get some dinner. I'd call "when" I found it.

I started my grid search a good 15 feet outside his suspected area. On my second pass in knee deep water, I got a banging signal. Dug a scoop of sand, shook it out in the ocean and heard the sound of solid metal rattling around in the scoop. Looked in the scoop and there was no doubt I had Phillip's ring. I was happy I started my search outside the area he thought it would be. Thankfully, he didn't sling his ring as far as it could have been either. I looked up the beach for Phillip, but he was just walking off the beach and didn't hear me holler at him. I think the search and recovery time was 2-3 minutes.

I walked off the beach and across the street to the rental house he was staying at with his friends. Philip and a few of his buddies were sitting out on the balcony when I crossed the street; they were all staring at me. I finished so quickly; I knew they were all wondering what was going on. Phillip had a strange look on his face until I held up my finger with his ring on it. I asked him if his ring looked like this. I think he flew down the stairs. He was one happy young man, and I'm sure his dinner tasted a whole lot better.

Found for New Yorkers

I got a call just before 3 p.m. from Katie. She told me that she was here on vacation with her husband, James, and their two sons from N.Y. Katie said she found one of my blogs, about finding lost rings, and wondered if I could help find James' wedding band. She went on to say that he lost it in the soft sand at Ocean Isle Beach, N.C. I asked a few of the usual questions, got the exact location to meet them at, and was on my way. This search sounded like it was going to be easy and fast. I always love these type searches. Dig, return, and go!

I got there in about 30 minutes and walked out on the beach. I was going to start searching and hopefully find it and surprise them with it when they showed up. Unfortunately, I had no idea where they had been sitting on the beach when they lost it, so I just waited.

It wasn't very long before I saw a man, woman, and two young boys walking down the beach access ramp behind a guy carrying a metal detector. I'm not too sure what I was thinking at the time. Maybe, by coincidence, another family had lost a ring and called somebody else to help find it. Once they crossed the beach access ramp, I recognized the guy with the metal detector as a friend. He just happened to be coming to the same area of the beach to do a little metal detecting on his own. He offered to help me, but I figured the area was small enough I wouldn't have too much trouble and thanked him anyway.

I met James and Katie and their two sons, and they explained what happened. I had the feeling they weren't too sure about this whole situation but were trying to stay optimistic. They showed me the small area the ring was supposed to be in, and I started my grid search. On the third pass, I got a great tone, looked up at them and gave them a big smile and dug a scoop. After spreading out the soft sand a couple of times, I finally eyeballed the ring, picked it up, blew off the sand, and handed it to James. Both he and Katie were happy to get his treasure back. Total search time was maybe 5 minutes.

I received the following from Katie on my post.

Thank you so much for your quick response and your service! We hope we will not need your services ever again but are thankful we found you and your blog!! We were amazed at how quickly you were able to find James' wedding band!

Slight Delay in Plans

James called me about 5:30 p.m. on March 16th saying he lost his wedding band in the sand and wondered if I was available to help find it. While we were talking I found out the resort; they were staying at, was in Myrtle Beach which is TRF Matt Fry's area. I called Matt, and he told me to go ahead and take the call. I called James back and said I was on the way. From his description of how and where he lost it, I'm thinking this is going to be another quick and easy find. This night was a special one for me, and I had plans, so I needed a fast search and return.

I raced to the resort and got there in about 25 minutes. I met James and his wife, Angelia, on the beach and we introduced ourselves. James and Angelia were here from Canada and on vacation with members of their family. James pointed out the small search area, and I started my grid search. On my first pass, I got nothing. About halfway through my second pass, I got the "tone." I dug a scoop of sand and dumped in on the beach. I looked down and saw his wedding ring laying in the sand. I picked it up, wiped it off, and handed it back to James. His and Angelia's excitement of getting his ring back is what this whole thing is all about. Handshakes and hugs! This search and recovery ended up being a short one which gave me plenty of time to do what I had planned.

Here is James' comment on my blog.

After having met Jim, I'm not surprised at how he downplays such an important find, given my family and I was returning to Canada 12 hours later, so there was absolutely no flexibility in the search. Or that he was there 25 minutes after I contacted him. Or that it was his wedding anniversary that day and that he was just about out the door for a celebratory dinner with his wife of 43 years and put everything on pause to help a complete stranger who happened across his name online.

Jim, we cannot say thank you enough again for your help during this minor crisis. Our apologies again to you and "Mrs. Jim" for catching you on your anniversary. And we've made sure the hotel is well aware of The Ring Finders in the event of any future similar situations from their guests.

Semper Paratus (Latin phrase, meaning "Always Ready." Official Motto of the U.S. Coast Guard)

Mothers Ring

Two hours from home after a week-long vacation, I got a phone call from Don asking if I could help find his wife, Diane's, Mothers ring that she lost around 8 p.m. the night before. We had a bad connection, so I told him I'd call him back around 2 p.m. and would be at his location between 4 and 5 p.m. During our conversation, I thought he gave me the name of a resort that it was in North Myrtle Beach.

When we talked at 2, he said the resort was in Myrtle Beach. I got all the details from Don and called Matt Fry, TRF Myrtle Beach. I knew Matt had also been out of town and wasn't sure if he was back home or not.

During Don's and my second conversation he told me that his wife lost her ring between 9 and 9:20 p.m. and not at eight like he initially said. With the change in time, I needed to leave home within the next 20 minutes to catch the tide. I tried calling Matt again, but he didn't answer, so I assumed he was still out of town and I left. I was within 15 minutes of arriving at the resort when Matt called back saying he was in town but to go ahead and take the ring call.

I arrived in the parking lot, and Don showed up shortly afterward to show me the exact area. Don explained that he and his family were down from Minnesota for the Myrtle Beach annual cheerleading competition. He was extremely pressed for time because one of his daughter's matches was within fifteen to twenty minutes. He had to leave so he wouldn't miss it and it was a good ten minutes to the convention center from where we were. Before he went, we agreed that I'd surprise Diane when I found her ring. I'm not sure if she knew that Don had contacted me to look for her ring or not. The plan was that I'd text him with a picture and then deliver the ring to the convention center. We had a plan set, so he pointed out the area and left me to do my search.

When I walked out on the beach it was packed with tourist and needless to say, I had an audience watching me search. People were curious, so they were asking questions like, "what are you looking for," and "what's the best thing you've ever found?" etc. I was nice and told them who I was, what I was doing, and answered their questions.

I finally got started on the search, and on my 4th gridline and calf-deep in the water, I got a strong signal. I looked at my display on the machine and had a solid 46-47. These numbers were what I wanted. There were other junk signals very close that I had to weed out. Luckily, I got the ring in the first scoop, dumped it out on the sand and immediately saw the gold. I got some cheers and applause when those watching saw me pick it up out of the sand.

I text Don with a picture, and he immediately replied with a 100% it's hers!!

I left the beach and the fanfare so I could get to the convention center. I'm not sure what Don had told Diane to get her out front away from her cheerleaders. Being one of the cheerleader moms, I knew she was busy trying to get the team ready and didn't have time for distractions. I think he told her I bumped their car in the parking lot or something like that, which would explain the unhappy look on her face when I met her. I told her that Don had called me and said that she had lost her Mothers ring. I asked her to describe her ring which would help me identify it. As she finished with her description, I held up her ring and said: "Does it look something like this?" Her expression was priceless, there were a few tears of joy, and the hugs were strong and sincere. She had to make a quick exit to get back to the girls, but she was one happy lady!!! She had her ring back, and their car was safe and undamaged.

Flew off Playing Volleyball

I got a call from Shana asking if I would help find a Silver Wedding Band lost in the sand at Sunset Beach N.C. I told her I'd be glad to help but I was currently at the movies with my wife, and I couldn't be there until about 10 p.m. She agreed to the time, and we hung up. After the movies, I called Shana back to let her know I was on my way and got the exact location where to meet. I dropped my wife off at home, grabbed my gear and headed for Sunset beach.

I arrived just before 10 p.m. and met Jake, who was the one that lost his ring, and his wife, Maria at the beach access path. On our way out to the beach, Jake told me that he was playing volleyball and when he hit the ball his ring flew off. He also gave me a description of the ring. Luckily, they had left the net up and set out small light loops in the area they thought the ring was. He let me know that about 15 family members had been digging through the sand in an attempt to find it. I let him know, just for future reference, that it's not a good idea to try and dig through the sand because you could be burying the ring deeper. What happens is that while the sand shifts back and forth, the weight of the ring makes it sink.

I started a north/south grid line, going from side to side, along the length of the net, and on the same side he had been on when his ring flew off. This area is where he thought the ring was, but I only found a few junk items and no ring. I then did an east/west grid over the same area and came up with nothing. I was getting a little concerned that all the digging buried the ring, but it should still be reachable with the detector. It was also possible that he flung his ring quite a distance from where he hit the ball.

I decided to expand my search and took a couple of steps outside the playing area next to the net pole on the far side. I made two steps in the new grid and Wham. I knew that I had Jake's ring. I took a shallow scoop, lightly shook out the sand, and there it was. I nonchalantly walked back over to Jake and asked him again to tell me exactly what he did when he felt the ring fly off his finger. I then asked him to describe the ring again. When he finished with his description, I held the scoop up to him and asked him if his ring looked like this one. Once he shined his flashlight into the scoop and saw his ring, he got an instant smile from ear to ear and so did Maria. How much better can it get than this! On the way back to the car, Maria let me know that they were leaving and heading back home the next day, so this was a Must find tonight. A perfect happy ending to their vacation with memories to share.

Overall, this was a simple search, but we were all surprised how far the ring flew from hitting the ball with an open hand.

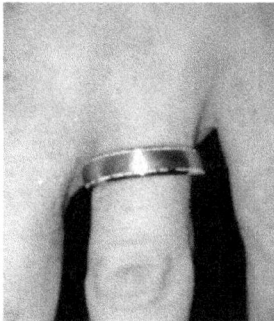

The Frisbee Did It

I got an email from Kevin about a lost wedding ring I had found and posted on Craigslist under "lost and found." Unfortunately, the ring I had didn't match Kevin's description of his ring. Going back and forth on email, I finally told Kevin I'd be glad to look for his ring. He was a little hesitant at first but agreed to have me try. We set it up that I'd be there the next morning.

I met Kevin the next day on the beach at 9 a.m. He told me that he and his family were here on vacation from Georgia. He went on to say that he was playing Frisbee with his sons on the beach the day before and in the process of catching the Frisbee he misjudged it. The Frisbee hit his finger, and he felt his ring fly off in a different direction than the Frisbee went

Keven showed me the area they had been playing in and the tides were low, so it should be a quick search. I set up a 30 X 60 ft. search area and started a north/south grid search that was parallel to the ocean. On the 6th pass, I got a good strong signal, dug a shallow scoop and dumped the sand on the beach. I spread the sand out with my foot and there it was. I don't think it took more than 30 minutes to find and return it.

I called Kevin letting him know I had it. I think it took him just about 2 minutes to come down from his room. He had a huge smile on his face. Got a big handshake from Kevin that made me feel that everything was alright now.

Kevin helped me out on finding his ring by getting landmarks and knowing the area he lost it in.

Quickies

Gold in the Sand for 3 Weeks

I received a late night email from Kristina on May 2nd. Her email said that she had lost her very sentimental wedding band on the beach at Ocean Isle, N.C. She also wrote, that she had been there during spring break and dropped it on Apr 12th. She asked, that if I thought it was worth it, she could email me a map with the exact spot. She finished her email saying to let her know if I was interested in helping. It was after midnight when I responded telling her that it was always worth it to at least take a shot at looking. I also included some questions in my response to where on the beach, what day and time, etc.

When I woke up the next morning, I checked my emails, and I had her response to my questions. She also said that she'd send me a map a little later that morning. I got her map around 9 a.m. that showed a satellite view of the beach with a little red dot marking the spot she lost it. Luckily, it was nowhere near the water. I grabbed my gear and hit the road for the 30-minute drive. The way I had it figured was her ring had been in the sand for three weeks. I had my fingers crossed on this one.

I got to the beach and found the area that she had marked. The satellite view with the little red dot on the beach was perfect. The search area was maybe 15 X 15 foot. I started a north/south grid in the dry sand. I was picking up a few targets, so the area hadn't been hunted too much. I think it was the 5th line when I got a good solid hit. I dug and shook a scoop of sand, and there was her little gold wedding band, about a size 5-6. She had also given me an inscription on the inside of the ring which I confirmed. We had a match!

I sent her an email from my phone, with a picture saying "Bingo!" She immediately called me. I could tell she was overwhelmed, by the sound of her voice, about getting her ring back. I was able to get her treasure in the mail that same day, and it was expected to arrive by that Friday.

On Friday, I got a text with her picture. She had the biggest smile on her face. I Love returning lost treasures!

Because of the satellite view, she sent with the area marked off, the search was fast and may have taken 15 minutes.

Kristina posted the following on my blog.

Jim,

Thank you again for doing the, what I thought, impossible. The ring has a lot of sentimental value, and I am really happy to have it back. Wish you good luck in finding the next lost ring.

Kristina

A Beautiful Sunrise

I got a call in the early evening on August 19th from Kevin, who with his family, was visiting from Va. He told me he was body surfing and was knocked into his daughter by a wave and felt his gold wedding ring slip off his finger. He said he pretty much gave it up as gone forever. A little later he saw how much difference there was between high and low tide and thought there might be hope. He found me through The Ring Finders site and asked if I could help try and locate it. I said, "Absolutely, I'll try and help."

He gave me the location where he lost it and a description of the ring. After checking the tide tables, I saw that the next low tide was at 5:33 a.m. So after doing the calculations of drive and search times, I told Kevin I'd be there by 4:30 in the morning. I also said that he didn't have to meet me there that early, I'd call him when I found the ring.

I set my alarm for 3 a.m., which is way too early and dark to start a search for a ring, but I had to take what I was given. I knew I wasn't going in the water, so I wasn't concerned. It was a good 45-minute drive, and I got there about 4:15 a.m. I stepped off the 75 yards Kevin said he paced from the dunes and added another 25 yards. Kevin also told me it was about 5-10 yards north of the stairs of the beach access and I made it 15 yards. Dragging my scoop behind me, I made a nice big search grid that put me right in the middle of the mid-tide line. I was getting wet, but I can handle ankle deep that early in the morning. I'm thinking this is a good sign and there is hope in finding this ring. Although it was too early for sunrise, it wasn't pitch black out there either.

After a north/south grid search, parallel to the ocean, I found nothing. I then started an east/west grid over the same area and on my first line, I decided to extend my search grid to the low tide line. Coming back up the beach on the 3rd line, I got the only signal I had and said to myself: "Oh Yeah!!" The ring ended up buried about 4-5 inches deep and about 105 yards from the dunes. Naturally, my headlamp batteries were too weak to show enough light, but luckily, I had grabbed a flashlight out of the car before I hit the beach. I lit up the scoop, and what I had matched his description perfectly. I took a picture of his ring with my phone and sent it and a text to him at 5:17 a.m. saying "Good morning, does this look familiar?" Got a response in about a minute saying "Incredible!" I text him that I was going to eat breakfast and I'd be back about 6:30, this would give him a chance to wake up.

When I got back, I saw him, his wife, Kristi, and two young daughters walking towards the beach. We introduced ourselves and then proceeded out to the beach so he and his kids could see where I found it. He told me that since he was getting his ring back, it was such a great start to the day that he and the family would watch the sunrise. And what a sunrise it was!!

Total search time was just about an hour.

Kevin added the following to my blog.

When I came up from a wave on Tuesday and noticed my wedding ring was missing, I immediately thought I would never see it again. I found the theringfinders.com site and found Jim's number and gave him a call. Spoke with him Wednesday night and before dawn Thursday morning he had it. My kids were amazed and had a great time retracing Jim's search area with him. Jim was professional, courteous, and responsive. It was a pleasure meeting him, and I am grateful for his finding my wedding band.

Help from a Little Hero

I was out on the beach one beautiful day, getting a little exercise and metal detecting the low tide line. A little 9-year-old young lady, named Gracie, came up to me asking if I had found a man's wedding ring. In the same breath, she said that her daddy had lost his. It's not uncommon to have children and adults come up and ask if I find things. This one felt different because Gracie's mother was right behind her. I heard her mom tell her that the ring was gone and not to bother the man. I introduced myself and said that I'm a member of "The Ring Finders," and I search and return people's lost rings and other items. I told her it's not necessarily gone and there's always a chance we can find it. I then asked her a few questions, "Where was he when it came off and what time did it happen?" She introduced herself as Lauren and said she wasn't with her husband, Matt when he lost it. She told me Gracie was and probably had all the answers. Gracie wasn't shy and told me he lost it about 4 p.m. the day before and then showed me the area. I got the ring description from Lauren, plus her phone number, and told her I'd text her when I found it. They were on their way back up to their room when Gracie saw me and came running, so they left me, to hopefully find their treasure.

I started a north/south grid search parallel to the low tide line just to eliminate that area before the tide started coming in. I then came back up the beach about 15 yards. On my first pass, I had a great signal, almost exactly where Gracie told me her dad had lost it. Two scoops and I saw Matt's wedding ring laying in the sand. I text Lauren with a picture of the ring and said

"Bingo!!! Look familiar??" Within a minute Lauren and Gracie were running out on the beach from the condo, with big grins on their faces. I got a big thank you from both of them and a big hug from Lauren. Come to find out, Lauren hadn't said anything to Matt about having someone look for his ring. Matt was still upstairs in the condo, so she was going to go back up and bring him down. We worked it out that we'd surprise him with his ring.

Probably about 5 minutes later, Matt and Lauren came walking hand in hand out of the resort and onto the beach. I walked up to Matt and said: "your wife told me that you lost something." He told me he had lost his ring in the surf the day before. I then asked him if he could describe what it looked like and where he lost it. He had both answers right, so I held out my closed fist and dropped his ring in his hand. He was so happy and amazed he had it back. He gave me a big handshake and Lauren got a big kiss from him!!!! Great big smiles from everybody.

Gracie was the real hero here! She's an intelligent young lady and without her details I know I'd of spent a lot more time looking for Matt's ring. Worse yet, if she hadn't come up and asked if I found a ring, I'd of never known there was a lost ring out there to find.

I received the following from Lauren on my blog.

Jim, you are an angel! We were mourning the loss of that ring and accepting the fact that it was long gone. Matt was truly heartbroken because it was his original wedding ring. Jewelry can be replaced, but that band stands for so much more to both of us. You've given us an irreplaceable gift, and we will be forever grateful. Yes, we have Gracie to thank, too. When we had given up, the faith and determination of a child delivered us a little miracle. Thank you so much, Jim!

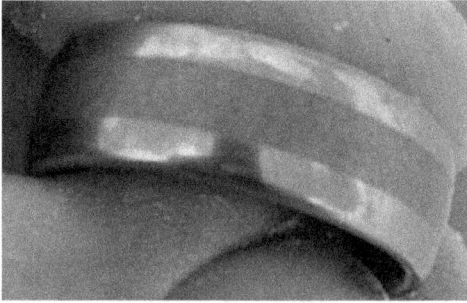

Small World

I got a call from Mary saying that she had put a post on Craigslist about her husband, Tim, losing his wedding band. She said she had gotten an email from someone referring me. That, someone, turned out to be my son-in-law.

I explained to Mary that I was a member of The Ring Finders and was an independent metal detectorist that could help find her husband's lost ring. She said that he had lost it at approximately 1 p.m. which was roughly 2 hours before high tide. She also mentioned that he lost it somewhere within a two-block area. This big of an area was going to be a tough search, but I agreed to meet them on the beach in about 15 minutes. I got the location, grabbed my gear, and was on my way.

When I arrived on the beach, I met both Mary and Tim. In talking to Tim, he explained what had happened when he lost his ring. Thankfully, he narrowed the search area down to about a 40-foot width and out in the surf about 30 to 40-feet. I was starting to feel a whole lot better about this search and thought there's a great chance of finding this one. I told them what I was going to do in the way of the search and told them they didn't need to stick around. It was getting close to dinner time, so I suggested they grab a bite to eat and that I'd call them when I found it.

I started a north/south grid search, parallel to the ocean, working the wet sand to make sure it wasn't there. After I knew the ring wasn't there, I changed my search to an east/west grid running from the wet sand out to waist deep water. On my sixth line, in thigh deep water, I get a signal on my PI. I took a scoop of sand, shook it out in the surf, and there's the ring staring back at me. I called Mary and had her verify the inscription in the ring, which was "4/16/16," the date they got married. I told her I had Tim's ring in my hand.

Mary said they'd be back in about 15 minutes, so I waited. When Tim and Mary showed up to get their ring they were both shocked and happy.

Tim and I started talking, and I told him I retired from the U.S. Coast Guard with 30 plus years of service. Ironically, Tim said his dad also retired from the Coast Guard. The more we talked, the more we realized that we had been in a few of the same places but not at the same time. Small world!

I received the following from Tim on my blog

So so so grateful to you Jim for finding my band and coming out so quickly. I really thought it was gone forever and kept replaying the ring tumbling off my finger in slow motion ala Frodo in Lord of the Rings. Our very serendipitous connection still blows my mind, and we will enjoy sharing this happy story for a long time. Big thanks to your son in law for recommending you to us. I hope our story helps other people reconnect with their lost treasures. Semper Paratus, thank you a million times over!

Tim and Mary

Teardrops in the Tides

Diaper and Memories out the Window

On January 27th, I noticed I had a missed call and a voicemail on my cell phone. The voicemail was from Brent, saying that he found me through The Ring Finders website and that his wife had lost a ring. He asked if I would call him back. When I called him, I got the full story.

He had taken his wife and very young son out to dinner the evening before. On the way home, his son had one of "those diapers," every parent knows what I'm talking about, one of those been there, done that, moments. Brent's wife, Allie was in the back seat and changed the baby. Unfortunately, it got to be a little overwhelming and Allie was compelled to toss it out the window. When she did, her beautiful 18K diamond clustered ring went with it. Allie commented to me, something like she never does anything like that, and losing her ring was punishment. Side note, the diaper did get picked up.

My understanding is they pulled over and immediately started searching for it. According to Brent, he went home and got a metal detector that he'd had as a boy. He also enlisted the help of his dad, Andy. He said they were out there searching along the side of the road, into the wee hours of the morning.

Brent text me the nearest address to the location and told me his dad would meet me out there. I plugged the address into my GPS and started the hour plus drive.

I got there a little before his dad and was driving slowly along the side of the road looking for a diaper. I finally parked and was walking along the road when his dad pulled up. I followed him down the road a little further where we parked, got out, and introduced ourselves. He walked me over to the spot where I started searching the ditch around the diaper. Andy was walking along the road looking for the ring, and in less than a minute, Andy said, "Look what I found." He was probably 10 feet from me and a foot off the road. I took a picture of the ring and sent it to Brent saying "look familiar" and telling him his dad found it. He quickly responded saying "Are u kidding me. That's great!" We worked it out that I'd drop it off at his house and surprise Allie. I followed Andy to Brent's house and waited about a minute for Brent to show up.

I met Allie and told her Brent had called me saying that she lost a ring and asked her to describe it to me. I had it on my little finger with my hand in my pocket, and as she's explaining it, I held my hand up in the air. She was very excited.

Lost Before the Big Day

The story begins when the love of your life catches you off guard one day. He drops to one knee, looks up at you and says those magical words: "Will you marry me?" The emotional tears start flowing down the cheeks, and you respond: "Yes!" He slips this fantastic ring on your finger, everyone oohs and aahs. There's big hugs, more tears, big smiles, and life is excellent.

Then one day, after you've been thinking about the upcoming big day, you glance down to look at your beautiful ring, and it's gone from your finger. Immediate panic sets in, tears start flowing for a whole different reason.

I can't imagine what that would feel like, but there's little doubt that it'd be devastating.

A 10 Year Wait

I received an email from Mandy asking if I might be able to help her find her engagement ring. Her email said she lost the ring in the surf on Saturday during her Bachelorette party. She also stated she had stayed in North Myrtle Beach, but the hotel she mentioned is in Myrtle Beach. I emailed her back asking her to call me so I could get additional details and confirm whether the hotel she had been staying at was in Myrtle Beach or North Myrtle Beach.

While I was waiting for her call, Matt Fry TRF Myrtle Beach called and asked if I had seen the listing on Craigslist about a lost engagement ring in North Myrtle Beach. After some discussion, we concluded that my email and the Craigslist posting was one in the same lost ring. Shortly after we hung up, Mandy called and gave me all the details which included the address of the resort. The resort was indeed in Myrtle Beach (Matt's area). She also mentioned in the phone conversation that her wedding was the following weekend. Ok, a little-added pressure, but we can handle it!

I called Matt back and after more discussion about me getting the call but it is in Matt's area we agreed to search as a team. I also let Matt know when her wedding was. Due to parking issues in Myrtle Beach, we met away from the beach and drove over together.

Mandy explained she was staying in one of the resorts with her mother, aunt, and a friend. When they decided to go out to the beach, they moved farther south because of the large crowds behind her resort. Unfortunately, there were 3 or 4 hotels associated with each other and all of them had the same name in some variation.

Matt and I showed up to the resort we thought it was and worked about 2 hours doing both north/south and east/west grids. We were leapfrogging each other working our way north along the incoming tide line. As a process of elimination, we wanted to make sure we covered as much as we could before the tide came in which would hamper our search areas. It had been cloudy and dark all day, then all of sudden the sky opened up, and it started pouring down rain.

As Matt was moving ahead of me, he was working the surf line with the incoming tide, while I was working the mid to high tide area. By now, we were both soaked to the bone. Matt was the smart one and had brought some rain gear; I was in shorts and a t-shirt. As hard as it was raining, Matt wasn't any better off than I was as far as staying dry.

After a few minutes, I glanced up at Matt and saw him coming out of the surf and walking up the beach with a scoop of sand. He looked at me and nodded his head. I knew he had the ring. He had the ring out of his scoop and cleaned off by the time I got to him. What a beautiful ring.

Matt and I were cold, soaked and hungry so we stopped for a late lunch and called Mandy. I put her on speaker phone as I told her we found her ring. In her mind, she knew the ring was gone forever, but was ecstatic and couldn't believe we had it. I took a picture of her ring and sent it to her and got the following text back "Omg!!!! That's my baby; God bless you so much!!!! You guys are truly Angels." I and Matt both love happy endings.

I put the ring in the mail the next day so she would get it in time for her wedding, which she did.

It's not often that I'm told the whole story about a lost ring, and it shouldn't be. When I get a call, my responsibility is to find the lost treasure. Mandy confided in me the whole story and said I could use it here.

Mandy's husband had had a massive heart attack when he was 26; he became so sick he lost his job. Later he was deemed medically disabled and no longer able to work. He had bought the ring when he could afford it and put it away until the day he would find a wife. Fast forward ten years when he and Mandy met. Soon after, he proposed to her and placed the gorgeous ring he had picked out years before, on her finger. Their moment in time was planned years ago without either of them knowing. Their love for each other would not waiver, even with the loss of the ring. The ring could never be replaced and by the Grace of GOD, it didn't have to be.

I received the following from Mandy in my post.

Jim & Matt,
I cannot begin to express how upset I was when I lost my ring. I tried to brush it off because it was only materialistic and we could replace the ring. As time went by, I thought of all the memories James and I shared, and the ring symbolized our start to a new & better life. I could not sleep thinking about how much I wanted my ring back and the memories we shared. I thank God you reached out to me. I prayed so hard for an Angel to please take my heartache away. You boys delivered a miracle! Your resilience and hard work are very much appreciated!! I could not believe how quickly you guys were to help me!! In less than 24 hours from hearing my cry for help, you were on the beach and searching. That is so rare to see individuals who care so much for others. I greatly value my ring, but I am even more grateful to meet people who have kind souls. Even if we were not able to find the ring, you guys are amazing!!! Thank you for taking time out of your day to search for me. I cannot express how much I am grateful for each of you!!!
Thank you.... Thank you..... Thank you!!!!

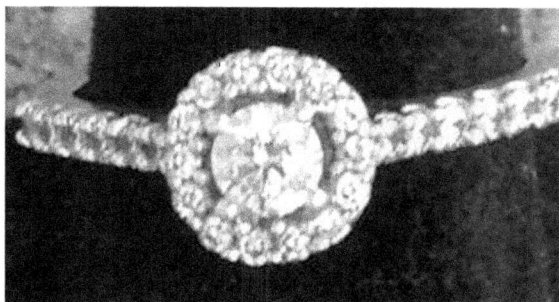

Lost Somewhere

I got a call from a young man saying his fiancé had lost her engagement ring at Carolina Beach, N.C. He said that they had been at the beach, then gone in town to one of the beach shops, then stopped for lunch and that's when she discovered her ring was missing. This search is one of those I really don't like because the ring could be in many places or none of them. On these type losses, I'm like the last resort, which is a very tough spot to be. Unfortunately, there wasn't a member of The Ring Finders in or around Carolina Beach at the time, and I was probably the closest one. Still, it's over a two and a half hour drive for me, one way. So with the trip up there, a three hour search and then drive back, it's easily an eight hour day. I'm a sucker and have a hard time saying no, so I agreed to try.

I met him in a parking lot because that particular beach they were on required four-wheel drive vehicle access only. He drove me down the beach to the spot they were.

I searched the area he said they were at with no luck. I went out at least another 20 to 25 yards on both sides. People moved their chairs, coolers, and umbrellas so I could search. I went all the way down to the mid tide line. I even did the parking lot from where they parked to the porta potties. Nothing!! He drove me back to my car, and as I got out of his truck, I did a quick check under the passenger seat and around the floorboard. I suggested when he got home he does a very thorough inspection of the inside of his truck. Never did hear whether he found it or not, I hope they did.

Found with a Friend's Help

I got a call on September 6th from Amy asking if I could help find her daughter, Adrianne's engagement ring. She said Adrianne lost her ring in the ocean during an incoming tide. After finding out the resort location, I was on my way and arrived in about 15 minutes.

I got there about 6:30 p.m. and found out Adrianne was on her way back home for work the next day. I met Adrianne's younger sister, Samantha (Sam), who gave me the details. Sam showed me the general area and explained how the ring disappeared. She also told me the ring was "silver" with a diamond on it. The story was that Adrianne was playing catch in about knee deep water an hour or so before high tide. Adrianne attempted to catch the ball, which she miscalculated just a little, jamming her ring finger and felt her ring slip off.

It turned out to be a long night, a couple of heavy storms with wicked lightning moved through, and I wasn't having any luck finding the ring. After 4 hours of grid searching north to south, east to west, and circular I called Amy and told her I'd be back around 7 a.m. the next morning. Thinking I was going to have to expand my search area quite a bit and that it probably wouldn't hurt to get some help. I emailed Matt Fry and Jim Brouwer asking if either of them would be available the next morning.

I got back the next morning at 6:45 a.m. and started another north to south grid. Around 9:30 a.m., after getting rained on again, I looked up to see Jim walking down the beach. At that point, I could have kissed him for showing up but refrained. There were far too many people sitting on their patios at the condos watching us. Anyway, I gave Jim the lowdown on where and what. Suggested he start looking in the area going north and I'd go south.

Two hours went by, and I see Jim walking towards me again, wasn't sure if he was calling it a day, which I doubted, or he found it. When he got to me, he asked if I was sure we were looking for a "silver" ring. He said he got a 12.04 hit on his machine. Owning a completely different type of machine, I had no idea what a 12.04 was. Jim informed me it wasn't "silver." Ok, so I asked him if he found it. He dropped a beautiful 14K White Gold engagement ring with what looked like a 3/4 Karat Diamond on it in my hand. Wow, my hero!! I asked where he found it and I'm almost positive I had gone over that area at least four times between last night and this morning. I did a quick test with my PI, and I got a very faint signal with the ring on top of the sand. I very well could have missed it buried the inch or so that Jim found it. My PI should have picked it up.

After thanking Jim at least ten times for his help, I slipped the ring over my little finger and dropped my gear off at the car. I found my way up to Amy and her husband, Brian's, condo room and knocked on the door. Amy came to the door, and I started giving her a sob story about how we've been searching for so long and that it was raining again and then I paused to let it sink in. Then I stuck out my hand with the ring and said: "And we found it"!! I can't describe her excitement other than to say it was awesome. Sam quickly text Adrianne who was busy at work. Another fantastic outcome thanks to a friend's help. Thank you, Jim Brouwer!

Lost Shortly After the "I Dos"

As the story continues, it's now the big day. You've been preparing for this day for a while. You're walking down the aisle. You exchange your marriage vows and place wedding rings on each other's fingers as a sign of your dedicated love for one another. What a great day!!!

Maybe within hours, days, or weeks, a ring is gone. You're not sure what to do, your world has collapsed. You console each other, saying "we'll replace it and everything will be alright." After all, it's just a materialistic item, right? In your hearts you know it can never be replaced, if it is, it will never have the same meaning.

Had it for a Few Hours

I got a call from Hunter about 3 p.m. concerning his lost wedding band and where he lost it. This one was in Myrtle Beach, so once again I called Matt, and he told me he had some things going on and to go ahead and take it. I called Hunter back, and we agreed to meet at 7 p.m. at his house.

Hunter and I met in his front yard, and he told me how he lost it. His and his wife, Michelle's, wedding bands were somewhat of a family heirloom, which had quite a story attached to them. The rings had belonged to his wife's aunt and uncle. Her aunt had passed the rings on to Hunter and Michelle as a wedding present.

Michelle and Hunter married on July 6th, 2017. Hunter's new wedding ring was too small for his ring finger, but with some help from family members he got it on. It was so tight that it became painful for him to wear. He was finally able to get it off and ended up wearing it on his pinky finger. At some point during the reception of their wedding and partaking of adult beverages the ring fell off his finger. He lost the ring in his front yard on the evening of his wedding day. Thankfully, it was a small front yard, but the ring had been lost for a little over two and half months by the time he called me. Hunter told me he had contacted another metal detectorist, not a member of The Ring Finders, a week after the loss who was unable to find the ring.

Hunter told me I was their last resort because their lease was up at the end of the month (6 days away) and they were moving. So I had a little leeway, if I needed it, to find the ring but I needed to get started with a grid plan.

Just before I got started on my search, Hunter handed me Michelle's ring. Her ring was smaller than his but an exact duplicate. I laid it on the grass and tested it with my machine and got a solid 53 on the AT Pro's meter. A 53 is in the range of a nickel and white gold. After about 45 minutes and finding a little trash and a buried nickel, I got a second nickel reading. I dug down through the grassroots and dirt to about 2-3 inches, and this time the "nickel" was Hunter's ring.

I cleaned it off and walked up to Hunter who was sitting on the porch. I was pretty sure he knew I had found it from the expression on my face. He asked me if I found it as I held it up and showed him his ring. He flew out of the chair and gave me the biggest bear hug I've ever had. He let me take the ring back so I could get some pictures while he ran inside to tell Michelle. She came outside in utter shock and more hugs. The feeling you get when getting this type of reaction is unbelievable. How can it possibly get any better than seeing this young couple so happy their treasure was back? Other than Michelle telling me she had just found out she's pregnant with twins. Wow!! What a Day!

Wore it for One Day

I received an email from Candy on June 22nd. She stated that she and her husband Charles had been in North Myrtle Beach on their honeymoon. He had lost his gold with diamond cut silver lining wedding band in the ocean in about waist deep water. She gave me the hotel name and a general idea of where the ring was in relation to the hotel.

I had a strong feeling this was going to be a rough hunt being in waist deep water. To confirm that hunch, Candy told me that the ring was lost ten days earlier on June 12th (one day after their wedding). I was currently out of town on vacation, and Candy and Charles were back home. I contacted Matt Fry in Myrtle Beach and asked him if he'd reach out to Candy and see if he could help her. He did, and he also received a couple of pictures of the ring, but due to his work obligations, he wasn't able to do an immediate search.

I returned home two days later and contacted Matt for an update on the ring. He said he wasn't able to search and sent me the pictures. The following evening I hit the beach at low tide and started the search without a more definitive area to hunt. After 3 to 4 hours of searching, it was getting dark, so I suspended the search and planned on getting out the next morning.

Early the next morning I showed up at low tide and expanded my search into the thigh to waist deep water. After about an hour in the water, I got a good strong signal, dug out three scoops of sand, and there was a man's wedding ring shining up at me through the shells.

When I found the ring, I wasn't sure it was the one I was looking for because in my mind I thought Charles' ring had diamonds on it. I continued searching, and after another 2 hours, I went home.

Once I got back home, I text Matt with a picture of the ring I'd found, saying I'd been out searching and found the ring in the photo. Matt text me back saying: "you found their ring, check their pictures I sent." Sure enough, I verified the ring with the pictures I'd received, and it was apparently a match.

I immediately typed up an email to Candy with pictures of me holding the ring and then I called her. She was elated as well as shocked that after two weeks her husband's ring was found. I wrapped the ring up with a couple of small shells, as a memento of their honeymoon vacation in North Myrtle Beach, and mailed it back to them.

Total search time was between 6 to 7 hours in the choppy Atlantic Ocean. After seeing the pictures of Candy and Charles that she sent me, I knew in my heart that the search was worth every minute.

Disastrous Honeymoon

I got a text message about 9:30 p.m. on July 4th. It stated that they had lost their wedding band and engagement ring set in the ocean earlier that day and to please call when I had the chance. I immediately called back and talked with Lyndsey. She said her and her husband, Joshua, have been married for just two weeks and they were on their honeymoon and "it's now officially a disaster." She gave me the hotel name and the address, and I was on my way. With it being the 4th of July, I knew the beach was going to be packed with both locals and tourist watching the firework displays. Parking was going to be a big problem. Surprisingly, I think I found the only remaining spot on the whole beach in one of the hotel parking lots and snatched it up. I was hoping my car would still be there when I was done and hadn't gotten towed someplace.

I met Lyndsey and Josh on the beach, and we walked down to the water's edge. She pointed out in the water, showing me about where she had lost it while playing catch. As she described it, "playing with a stupid little yellow ball they bought." Lyndsey said she was in water up to her thighs when she felt the ring fall off after catching the ball. She showed me a picture of her beautiful ring set. It was a two-piece set in which the engagement ring sat inside the wedding band.

I was faced with a little bit of a dilemma because the tide was still high and my go-to machine, for water hunting, is my PI. I'd been having quite a bit of problem with that machine and had it back in the shop for repairs. My AT Pro can't get wet much above the coil but is great in the wet and dry sand. I was making the best of it but getting a lot of false target hits and not making any progress. After about 30 minutes, I got out of the water and moved back to the wet sand and started another north/south grid search, following the tide out. After 3 hours of searching, I came up empty and called it a night at 1 a.m. I stayed up most of the night trying to figure out a better game plan for finding her ring at the next low tide.

I sent Lyndsey an email early in the morning, asking for a little help. Looking at the tide tables for the 4th and 5th, I asked her if she would go into the water at 10:55 that morning, which would be at mid-tide. I asked her to walk out to waist deep water and then pace off the number of steps, back up the beach, to a stationary item. The only stable thing on the beach was the beach access sign, which worked out well. She gladly complied. Around 10 a.m. I got a call from Matt Fry, TRF Myrtle Beach, saying he'd received a text from a girl who had lost her ring in North Myrtle Beach and was passing it off to me. After comparing the text messages, we realized both came from Lyndsey, who was trying to cover all her bases to get some help. Talking with Matt, I told him about my PI, and he offered up his CTX 3030, which I quickly accepted. I had never used that particular machine before, but I discovered it takes some practice to learn how to use it properly.

The temperature for the day was forecast to be above 100 degrees. Considering the search area, I got to thinking, with some help we could cover twice the space in half the time. It would help get us out of the heat quicker. Unfortunately, things don't always work out as planned!!! I talked to Jim Brouwer to see if he would be willing to help. As always, he was raring to go; GOD bless him!!!

We met on the beach at 1 p.m., and I marked off the 105 steps, baby steps for me, that Lyndsey had done earlier. Now we're within ten feet of the lifeguard chair that was sitting right in the middle of our search area. Jim and I did grid searches in all four directions for a good three hours with very few targets and no rings. Finally, Jim moved closer to the lifeguard chair and BAM! I heard him holler at me and as soon as I looked over at him, I immediately recognized his expression. I walked over, and he dropped the ring in my hand – Uh oh! He only had the wedding band without the engagement ring. The rings came apart at some point, and the engagement ring was not attached. We figured the engagement ring had to be within inches of the wedding band. We dug out his 5 inches round by 3-inch deep hole into a 3 to 4 foot round by 2-foot deep hole. Nothing!! We did another 10 X 10-foot grid search around the hole that included moving the lifeguard stand, with the life guard's permission of course. We then expanded our grid search again to cover a 20 X 20-foot area and still got nothing. We rechecked all the low, water-filled runnels and holes close to where Jim found the wedding band and came up empty. We knew the engagement ring had to be there somewhere, but after another hour we came up blank. We figured the engagement ring had separated from the wedding band and because of the diamond, settled in the sand while the round wedding band rolled around and then sank. So now, it's just a matter of finding where the engagement ring settled. I was hoping that there'd be a part 2 to this story. I have gone back about every week for the rest of the summer, hoping for some beach erosion. The erosion never happened, I still think of her ring. I doubt anybody found it; I just think it got buried by the sand.

After all that searching, I hated telling her that we had only found part of her set. Reluctantly, I took a picture of her wedding band and sent it to Lyndsey with an explanation that we couldn't find her engagement ring. I quickly got a response of "oh, my gosh!!!!" We met later and although we hadn't found the engagement ring she was still happy. She said, "The wedding band signifies the married and is what it's all about."

Lyndsey posted the following on my blog.

Jim,

I can't tell you over and over again how amazing you are! My whole family is still in awe that we have my wedding band! When I received the text message from you with the picture of my wedding band – many of us were speechless. I am blessed beyond measure to have been able to come across The Ring Finders! What you guys do is phenomenal! My thought process of calling you was that I was so incredibly thankful that you would come out, but I really did not have a lot of hope. I just didn't want to leave without a fight when it came to losing my ring set. But I still just can't even put into words my thankfulness to you. You showed up 20 minutes after I called you and the type of person that you are showed from the first time I met you. It was pretty reassuring to have such a wonderful person (trustworthy) searching for it. Josh and I are forever grateful. And we're grateful you feel as though you haven't given up on my engagement ring!!! Lyndsey

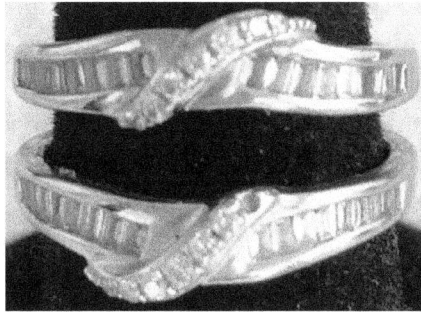

Three Week Anniversary

I got a call from Jodi, who was here on vacation with her family from S.D. She asked if I could help find a Wedding and Engagement ring set lost in waist-deep water in Myrtle Beach. Again, I had to clear it with Matt. I called Matt who was busy and told me to go ahead and take it.

I called Jodi back, got the resort location and was on my way. I arrived within 20 minutes and met Jodi, her brother, mother, father, and Sister Jenna, and Jenna's husband, Clayton, on the beach. I found out that Jenna was the one who had lost her ring set and I could tell she was very distraught. It was also her and Clayton's three week anniversary.

I got some additional details on the time, area, and the depth they were when the rings came off. I found out that Jenna, her husband, and brother had been body surfing when she felt her ring slip off her finger.

I started a grid search in knee deep water with my PI, which I've been having problems with on and off all summer and had just gotten it back from being repaired. About 25 minutes or so in the water and the PI started acting up again with a low volume and one steady tone. Having a defective detector is not good when I'm looking for someone's treasure!!! Luckily, I had brought my AT Pro as a backup just in case. It was a good thing I did.

Thinking I'd have to work in the water, I knew my machine would work but it wasn't the best in the conditions I was facing, I needed help. So as a precaution, I called Jim Brouwer telling him the situation and asking if he could help, as always he was on his way. In the meantime, I let Jenna know what was going on with my machine and me calling Jim. I planned on going ahead and starting a grid search at the tide line and work my way out as far as I could until Jim showed up. As I got to the water line, I moved farther south than where they told me she lost her ring. I extended my search area to my usual 10-15 yards trying to figure out my starting point for the grid. As I started my search, I took two steps and got a good 46-47 (perfect numbers for a small white gold band) on the screen of my machine, and I'm thinking there's no way. I took a scoop of sand and dumped it on the ground and could see Jenna's beautiful ring set looking up at me, glimmering in the sunlight. I'm chuckling as I pick it up and walk out to the surf to wash the sand off the rings.

I slipped her rings into my pocket, knowing they're hers from the original description I got. I called Jim and told him thanks, but I had found them. I then walked back up the beach to where Jenna and her family were, poor thing; she was so upset. I asked her to tell me one more time about her rings. She said she had pictures on her phone and started looking for her phone in her purse. Clayton was standing beside me, and I gave him a peak of her rings in my cupped hand as Jenna was looking for her phone. After a few seconds, I jokingly tell her she's taking too long and does it look like this as I hold her ring up. Jenna looked up, saw her rings, and instantly covered her face with her hands trying to hold back her emotions. The excitement everybody had was unbelievable. Jenna and Clayton's three week anniversary will be one they will never forget.

I received the following comments from Jenna and her mother in my blog comments.

What began as our first family vacation in years quickly turned the corner when I lost my wedding ring in the Atlantic Ocean 15 minutes into our trip while surfing... I thought tonight while in Myrtle Beach we would be celebrating completing the first year of Nurse Practitioner school, surviving a day of surfing, or just being together as a family.... After hours and hours of walking the beach and several tears being shed, we gave a desperate plea of googling and coming across a local "ring finder." Turns out Jim from The Ring Finders of North Myrtle Beach SC was my saving grace!! He came immediately following our phone call and swept the water up and down and back and forth with his metal detector. Not only did he give me reassurance and confidence that he would find it, even if it meant searching for weeks, he gave me evidence...MY RING!!!!! Most people do not know people like Jim are out there ready to help out of the pure goodness of their hearts and with very little recognition! So if you're ever in my position... First, take your ring off before you get in the water or know people like Jim are out there just waiting to help!!! Thank you, Jim!!!!

Jim was amazing!! I wouldn't have believed it, but I saw it with my own eyes!! My daughter lost her wedding ring while surfing (she has only been married three weeks). Jim was prompt in his arrival to the beach, very friendly and determined to recover the ring!!! He found the ring in less than one hour!!!! Thank you, Jim!!!

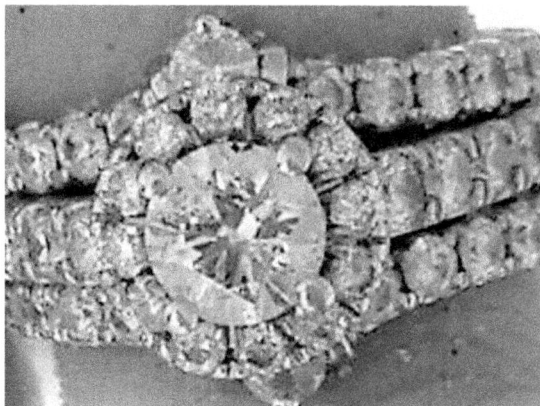

Tough Searches with Mixed Results

It's time for that family vacation; a year or two in the planning. Families arrive at the beach ready for some good times. They're all checked in at the hotel, grab the towels and walk out on the beautiful sandy beaches. Mom removes her rings to apply the suntan lotion to the whole gang. She either puts her rings on her lap or puts them in her purse. They spend a few hours having a great time, then they pack up, and mom can't find one of her rings.

Another scenario could be that dad is playing with the kids in the sand or surf, having a great time. They might be throwing a ball, building a sand castle, or just enjoying the ocean. All of a sudden, dad felt his ring slip from his finger, and watched as it disappeared into the sand or surf. These things happen every day along the beach. The vacation they've been waiting for is now destroyed. The couple spends hours trying to find the ring to no avail. Unfortunately, many couples go home without their treasure.

Once in a while, I'll get a call from one of these couples and can return their treasure before they go home. Then there are other calls I get that I know are going to be tough ones. The couples have returned home and can't give up on their lost ring. They try last-ditch efforts in hopes of finding a miracle.

They stumble across The Ring Finders and make a desperation call. These type searches are always hard when someone lost an item days or weeks ago. Worse yet, the owner isn't sure where it could be. There have been occasions when the beach conditions were horrible with additional sand, or someone found the item before I got there. Not all the results are bad, and I have had a good percentage of the items found, persistent pays off. The treasures I can't locate are heartbreaking, but there's little I can do other than look. One thing I promise the owners when they ask for help is that I will give a 100% effort in trying to find their item. I don't give up a search until I'm positive I've searched every bit of the presumed area. I wish I could recover them all, so their stories continue.

Delayed by a Storm

I got a call from Holli asking if I could help her friend, Kandi, find her lost engagement and wedding ring set. She stated Kandi had put the ring set in a beach bag and left it sitting on the beach. The bag had gotten blown over by a pretty good wind gust, which tossed the ring set into the sand where it disappeared.

I was right in the middle of something that I couldn't break away from when Holli called. I told her that I wouldn't be able to get to the beach for about an hour, and I'd call her when I got there. There was a very heavy thunderstorm going through the area at the time, so that also delayed me a little bit.

I finally got to their location and called Holli. The storm was still pretty intense and kept me from starting the search. There was a lot of lightning associated with the storm that was coming straight down to the ground. I wasn't about to go out on the beach. I met Kandi, her husband Bill, Holli, and her husband, Seth, under cover of their condo where it was safe. In the course of us talking, I learned that they were here from W.Va. on vacation.

We started talking while we were waiting for the storm to pass, Holli told me that Seth and Bill had rented a metal detector and attempted to find the rings themselves, with absolutely no luck. She then googled "how to find a lost ring in Myrtle Beach," and one of my blogs from The Ring Finders website popped up. She said it was a shot in the dark when she called me. I thanked her for calling and then explained that the rental metal detectors around the area are inexpensive detectors. Those machines aren't built to work in the salt water or wet sand because of the mineralization that gives all kinds of false readings. I told them the detectors might work in the dry sand but are sketchy at best. I also said, if you're unfamiliar with a metal detector or how to set them up right, that you might get lucky and find your item. If you weren't sure, more likely than not, you're wasting your time and money.

After about 30 minutes, the storm finally passed through, and I could start my search. Kandi gave me a full description of the rings and showed me the area she thought the rings would be. I expanded her search area and started my grid search. After about 40 minutes, I had to increase the search area out a little further, and within a couple of minutes, I got a strong signal. I took a small scoop of sand, very lightly shook it out, and there was this beautiful ring. It was a perfect match to what Kandi had described.

I glanced over at Kandi, who with Bill, Holli, and Seth had been watching me as I was searching. I gave Kandi a wink, a little smile, and nod for her to come over. Not knowing what I was up to, she sheepishly made her way over to me. I held the scoop out so she could look in it and BOOM, she saw her ring. She reached in the scoop and grabbed her treasure and gave me a huge hug and her tears started flowing. The other 4 of us were caught up in the moment and shared the return.

Family Referral

I received an email through my email address at The Ring Finders website at about 9:30 p.m. from Chad. His email said he had lost his wedding ring, four days earlier, while swimming in the ocean during high tide. He went on to tell me that the ring was very sentimental because it had belonged to his grandfather and it had been passed down to him. He described the ring as a gold wedding band with six small diamonds that were evenly spaced, across the top of the ring. He also thought it was 10K but wasn't 100% sure. He requested that if I find the ring or know of anyone who might have found it, to please call him. Chad finished the email saying that there had been a gentleman on the beach metal detecting when he lost it, and he had asked the man that if he finds it to, please call him.

I checked the tide table for the area and saw that we were just about at the right time, tide wise, to search. I responded back to Chad advising him that I'd be willing to help him if he'd like. I also told him that although it was getting late, I could be there within 15 minutes and catch the outgoing tide. In a follow-up email from him, he stated he'd like to have me look for it. He provided me with the details of the location and away I went.

Chad and his family were out enjoying the sites of Myrtle Beach, so I got there before he did. I had some real concerns with trying to find this ring. For one, it's been out in the sand for four days or 8 tide cycles. Secondly, we've had some big storms go through the area in the last couple of days. Lastly, and probably, more importantly, there was someone in the area metal detecting that knew there was a lost ring there and had all kinds of time to find it. None of these scenarios were very conducive to me finding this ring. But I was up for the challenge to at least try.

I started searching in the area I thought Chad had described in his email. It wasn't too long before he showed up and got me on track, needless to say, I was off about 25-50 yards. As we were walking towards the new search area, I asked Chad where he was from, and he told me W.Va. I mentioned that I had found a young lady's ring the night before, who was also from W.Va. He replied that Kandi was his sister-in-law. So, she must have shared her story with the rest of the family. He lost his ring three days before she did but she got hers back first. Ok, now I had double the pressure, not only was I looking for a family heirloom but I couldn't do for one family member that I couldn't do for the other.

I started searching at the low tide line doing a grid search back up the beach to the mid tide line. It was getting late so I told Chad that I'd call him when I finished for the night or I found it. He agreed and went back to his room. I worked my grid for about an hour and a half finding all the typical beach junk. Right around 11:15 p.m. I finally got an excellent signal. The target was buried and took a few scoops of sand to undercover it. I finally got the target out of the hole and laid the sand on the beach. I spread the sand out with my foot, turned on my headlamp and there was a man's gold wedding band just lying there so handsomely. I was very confident I had the right one. I picked it up, washed it off in a little pool of water, and looked for the details of the description I had gotten from Chad. GOT IT! I had Chad's grandfathers and now Chad's wedding ring in my hand. What a great feeling. Now for the shock factor. I called Chad, figuring he was probably in bed but he answered his phone right away. Since I wasn't sure where his room was, I asked him if he could meet me in the garage parking lot. I'm sure he thought I'd finished for the night. After a few minutes, he showed up. I just held out my closed hand with the ring in it; when he held out his hand, I laid his ring in it. I don't think Chad is a man of many words or much emotion, but he was shocked that I found it. Another vacation memory!!!!

Thanks to Holli for not only helping Kandi get her ring back but also helping Chad find out about The Ring Finders and getting his ring back as well.

A short time later I received the following email from Jaime, Chad's wife

Jim,

You are a kind, amazing man!!! A man of many miracles, an angel on earth!!! I cried when my husband showed me his lost ring that you found after 4 days and heavy storms!! When he lost it, I didn't think we would ever see it again! I wish I would have been there to personally give you a hug!! What you do is wonderful, and I am thankful for your help!!! Thanks so much!!!

Donnie's Find

On July 10th, 2015 I received a call from Scott stating he had lost his wedding band in the Ocean and wanted to know if I could help. I started asking Scott the obvious questions of what time he lost it, how deep in the surf he was, etc. There was no way I wasn't going to help him, but I had a medical issue. Two days earlier, I had had three separate surgeries at one time, none of them serious. Unfortunately, though, the doctor had me on a lifting limitation of nothing heavier than a jug of milk and I could not get any of the areas wet and risk infection. So, my restriction was about knee deep water which was going to be tough with him losing his ring in the ocean.

When I talked to Scott, he said that he and his family were headed back home to Charlotte, N.C. He put me in touch with his parents, Bud and Martha, who were staying a few extra days on vacation. I got their location and met up with them on the beach about 9 p.m. They showed me the area Scott lost his ring in which just happened to be in the water. Things weren't looking good for me as far as the depth of water I needed to search. I searched out to about thigh deep water and started getting some bigger swells that were getting to close to my wounds.

After doing about as much as I could, I contacted my son-in-law, Donnie, who had never metal detected before and asked if he could help. He showed up in about 15 minutes, and I started running him through the process of using my White's PI machine. I laid targets in the sand for him to interpret and showed him how to do a grid search.

About an hour of watching him search the surf and coming up empty, I brought him back in and relieved him and started searching the low tide line towards the high tide line. At this point, it's about 10:30 p.m., very dark and I'm thinking of calling it for the night and returning at low tide the next morning.

I was talking to Bud and Martha and decided I'd work a little further up towards the high tide line when my son-in-law spoke up and said: "I'll do it." So I stepped back and let him go, at this point, I think that I had created a monster. And what a monster he turned out to be, about his third pass in the grid I was watching his face and then saw him dig up a scoop full of sand. I walked over and showed him how to dump the sand out of the scoop, spread it with his foot and narrow his target area. Soon as he did, the flashlight picked up a small round object, and there was a wedding ring. I verified the inscription that Scott's wife Diane said would be inside the ring and we had the right one. Bud and Martha were speechless and very excited we found Scott's ring.

I called Scott and gave him the good news. His response was priceless, so was Diane's which I heard through the phone. Scott told me to go ahead and give it to his father, and he'd get it from him, which I did. Luckily, Scott's ring wasn't lost as deep as I thought...

Someone Picked it Up

I got a call from a lady that was visiting with two of her girlfriends and had lost her wedding band. She had lost it a few hours before she realized it. She called me and said she was sure she lost her ring in the dry sand. I got the resort name and location and headed out. I thought this should be a pretty straightforward search, recovery, and return.

I got there within 10 minutes and met her in the dry sand area where she said she had lost it. She said that she had taken her rings off and put them in her lap to apply lotion and then moved them to her bag. A short time later, the three ladies picked up their beach chairs and went down the beach closer to the water between the mid to low tide line. When they came back to their towels and bags they left in the dry sand; she grabbed her rings and jewelry from her beach bag. She put everything on but her wedding band, she searched everywhere and everything, but couldn't find it. She thought that maybe the ring got stuck in her lap and when she stood up it flipped into the dry sand.

The search area was small, maybe 10 foot by 10 foot and they still had their chairs and bags in the search area. They helped me move everything out of the way. I searched the area and didn't find anything. I kept extending my search area further and further out and was finding things like bottle caps and pull tabs but no ring. I double checked and tested a couple of her other rings and was getting good signals on my detector. I was confident her wedding band was not in the area. I had her empty her bag of all its contents and looked through all of them, one by one. I then ran the detector coil over her empty bag, thinking maybe the ring could have slipped through a tear in the lining. Her ring was nowhere. I started to grid down to the area they moved to at the mid-tide line, still nothing. After a couple of hours of searching and watching the tide come in, there wasn't much more I could do at the time. I told her I'd be back the next day at low tide and try again.

I showed up the next day and found her and her friends in the same area of the beach. I asked her if there was anything else she might have remembered during the night. She said yes, and explained that while they were sitting down by the low tide line, they had been keeping their eyes on their bags. She said they noticed other people sitting close to their area. They observed one of the people walk about 5 feet from their bags, reach down, and appeared to pick something up and walk away. At the time, she didn't know her ring was missing, and the three of them didn't have any concerns because the person didn't disturb their property. With everything she told me the day before about having the ring(s) in her lap, it just didn't make sense that her ring wasn't there. We all concluded that more likely than not, a person saw her ring sitting on top of the sand, picked it up, and walked off with it. It was a sad situation, but it happens all the time.

Stuck in the Mud

I got a call from Heidi on Sunday, August 28th after she found me in The Ring Finders website directory. She asked if I could help find a toe ring she lost while in the mud and water with her sister-in-law, Jennifer. She went on to say they had been swimming in the Intracoastal Waterway at Holden Beach N.C. Heidi told me that her specially made ring was from another ring that had been given to her and was very sentimental. She also said she noticed her toe ring was gone after her foot had sunk up to her ankle in the mud as she was leaving the water. She gave me the area she lost it in, so I checked the tide table and saw I had a small window of opportunity before low tide and started the 45-minute drive. My first search in the Intercostal Waterway, and in retrospect, it was probably one of my hardest searches yet.

When I arrived at the spot, it was around 10 p.m. and pitch black. I had my headlamp on and noticed there were broken clam and oyster shells all over the beach. With every step, I was getting stuck in the mud up to at least my knees. I searched for about an hour and a half from the high tide line to mid-tide line and called it a night.

The next day I arrived a little before low tide and noticed that Heidi had put signs up on two trees in a little park area on the day she lost her ring. The signs said who she was, her phone number, what she lost, and where she lost it in. The area she lost her ring was between the two trees. I searched for an hour and a half and again knee deep in mud. My feet were getting pretty cut up from the shells, and I still wasn't having any luck. At some point, the mud literally sucked my sandals off my feet as I was doing my search. What made it worse is I couldn't find or recover them out of the mud, they just disappeared! This search was turning out to be a mess with this soft mud.

I decided to run to a local sports store and pick up a pair of hip waders and give it another try. Two days later I was back, and the hip waders worked great, but I still wasn't finding the ring. I did, however, see both of my sandals laying on top of the mud, strange how that happened. I called Heidi telling her I wasn't having any luck in finding her ring and wasn't sure I was searching in the right area. Heidi said that Jennifer was going to be back at her beach house that weekend. I suggested that Jennifer meet me either Saturday or Sunday to give me a more exact area where the ring was.

Jennifer met me on Sunday during low tide. She showed me the area she thought Heidi's ring was lost in but thought Heidi might have lost it in the mud and not the water. Jennifer had me about 10 to 15 yards north of where I had been searching. I had my PI and my waders and decided to start my grid in the far left corner of the new search area. I went straight out to knee deep mud and water, getting stuck with every step. I worked the grid from the shore to the water and back. The first target was in the mud and was a fishing weight. I walked out to about upper calf depth and got a second target, as I'm separating the thick mud with my fingers in the scoop I hear the clank of something metal – Well I'll BE!!! I washed the ring off and walked back up to Jennifer, who was sitting on a small seawall with a friend of hers that she brought along. Luckily, she had stuck around. I walked up to her and said: "boy these conditions are horrible." I know Jennifer thought I was all finished until I stuck my closed fist out to her and dropped Heidi's ring in her hand. I love seeing the expressions on people's faces when I give them back a lost treasure. Although it wasn't Heidi, Jennifer did a good job showing her excitement for Heidi.

I took a picture of the ring and sent it and a text to Heidi saying "Surprise!" I think it took Heidi less than 10 seconds to call me. She couldn't believe it. Heidi told me to go ahead and let Jennifer have the ring, and she'd get it back from her.

Heidi had to wait a few days before she got her ring back but she knew for sure it was on its way.

Thank you, Jennifer, for putting me in the right spot which was a tremendous help, huge time saver, and a great success.

I received the following from Heidi in my blog comments.

I know we have all had those moments in our lives where we would like to have a "Do-Over"! A moment where you would have done something differently, but we don't always get that chance. Well, this time I did get that chance. Jim Wren gave me that chance. My Guardian Angel! I was near Holden beach and had taken off all my jewelry except a gold toe ring. Which I never take off. I had not even remembered quite honestly that it was on. This was a ring that had been made for me from another special ring. This was irreplaceable! I found Jim's name on the ring finders.com, and that's where and when my Do Over began. Jim made me feel so good with each and every conversation. I had resigned myself to having lost my ring. But Jim's focus was never how much he was getting paid but finding what meant so much to me. It was so obvious that he was passionate about what he did in helping people. He was relentless going repeatedly to the beach for over a week. Never seeming to give up! For that, I am eternally grateful!

Thank you, Jim!

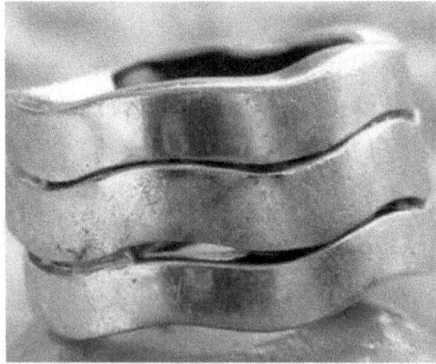

31st Wedding Anniversary

I got a call from Amanda on Thursday, August 11th asking for help in finding her husband's gold wedding band. She went on to say they were on a little vacation from Greenville, SC and celebrating their 31st wedding anniversary. I was on my way back from out of town and told her I'd call her when I got close, and we could meet on the beach.

About an hour later, I met up with Amanda and John to get the details on exactly what happened and learned John had been tossing a volleyball back and forth with their daughter Presley when he felt his ring come off. They showed me where they had been sitting and where John and Presley had been playing in the shallow water that was now completely underwater with the incoming tide. Knowing that I was going to do some water searching and not having my water machine that was back in the shop for repairs, I contacted Jim Brouwer and asked if he had a water machine I could borrow. Once again Jim came through and gladly loaned me his Gold Quest SS PI. While I had him on the phone, I asked him if he wanted to tag along, which he gladly accepted. While waiting for Jim, I checked around where John and Amanda had been sitting and a little bit of the tide line with my AT Pro just to rule those areas out. Once Jim got there he gave me a quick lesson on his Gold quest PI and then we decided we'd come back in a few hours and work the outgoing tide.

Jim got back to the spot a few minutes before I did and started working the water line up towards the dry sand. I tuned on my (new) PI machine, made a few practice runs with it, and started working from Jim's first line seaward. Eight grid lines and 30 minutes later my new water machine gives me a banging signal, one scoop and up comes John's Gold wedding band. I took a picture of me holding John's ring and sent it with a text saying BINGO!!! Uh oh, Amanda's not calling me back. I gave her a few minutes and called her, when she answered, I ask her if she had seen the text I sent. She checked, and I could hear her say "He found it!!!" They were on their way back to their resort but made a U-turn and arrived back on the beach in about 5 minutes. I could tell by their faces that not only could they not believe the ring had been found but were trying hard to contain their emotions. I LOVE returning people's treasures!!!!

John and Amanda, Happy 31st Anniversary and may you celebrate many more in the company of John's ring on his finger.

I received the following from Amanda and Presley on my blog.

From Amanda

My husband and I were on vacation in North Myrtle celebrating our anniversary. My husband and daughter were tossing a ball back and forth in the surf, and shortly afterward we realized his wedding band was missing. We looked, to no avail, and considered the ring a loss. We were almost sick the rest of the afternoon, but I thought I would put an ad on Craigslist "lost and found" in case an honest person found it. While I was making the post, I saw an ad for TheRingFinders. I was skeptical but thought it was worth a shot. I called Jim Wren, and he put me at ease right away. He was very professional when we met to show him the area where we thought the ring was and told me he would call if he found it. I really didn't expect to hear from Jim, but around 7:00 that afternoon he sent a text with a picture of him holding the ring!!! Our prayers were answered, and we couldn't be more excited to go meet him to get the ring. I would recommend him to anyone who has lost an item-he seemed genuinely concerned about us and our feelings. I can't thank him enough!!

From Presley

While playing volleyball with my dad in the ocean, his wedding band flew off his hand, and we didn't realize it until we were headed back. The tide had started to come in, making our "volleyball court" underwater and waaay too difficult to search. After tracing our steps, we left. My mom was going to put an ad on craigslist for it, but saw an ad for "the ring finders of north myrtle beach" after speaking to a man named "Jim," he told us he could come out and meet us at the beach. He showed up on time and had his equipment with him. We let him know where we sat and where we had been throwing the volleyball. He searched where we had sat with no luck. He told us to wait until six o'clock when the tide was low, and he'd come back. While eating, we got a call from him, and he'd found the ring! He said it was right where we had been throwing the ball, and said he spent about 30 minutes looking for it. My dad, mom, Mimi, and I were amazed that he could find it, despite being through low and high tide twice. EXTREMELY impressed with this business, and would recommend it to anybody vacationing in Myrtle who's dropped any items in the sand. Jim was a very nice guy, who works on a reward basis, he also donates 10% to Saint Jude's Children's Hospital. #blessed

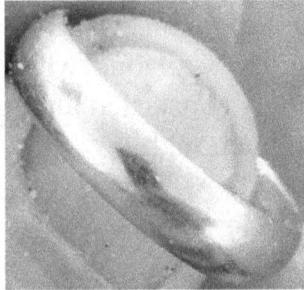

Beyond the Sandbar

I had a call from a man who had found me while searching the internet for a way to find his lost ring. He told me he had been in the ocean when it came off and described his ring as a silver ring with a blue star sapphire stone. He gave me the time he lost it, which turned out to be low tide. He also told me that he was about chest deep. Ok, with the details he gave me, I felt this was going to have little to no chance of being found. I'll always give it a try though. The next low tide was at 2 a.m., and there was no way I was going out to chest deep water at low tide in the pitch blackness of night. There's big fish in the Atlantic Ocean, and some of them eat people, I was not going to become a statistic. So the next opportunity would be the following day at about 2:30 p.m. which was a lot more realistic. At least I'd be able to see what might be swimming around me. We set it up that I'd meet him on the beach behind his resort at 2 p.m. which would allow me to work the incoming tide.

We met at 2, and he showed me the landmark he had picked out when his ring came off. Turned out to be a window of one of the rental properties. Him pointing out his marker helped a little to put me in a manageable search area, but not much. He said he was in chest deep water, so I had another problem. He was probably 6 foot 4 or so, and I'm 5 foot 10 1/2, which meant that his chest deep put me under water. The situation was getting worse by the minute. I made it real clear to him that there was little chance of finding his ring, which he readily accepted. By him being out as deep as he was, he was beyond the sandbar. When the waves hit the sandbar, it's pretty intense. So anything lost that far out is going to get bounced, pushed, and moved around violently.

I made my way out as far as I could go and still be able to bob in the surf. I wasn't finding anything. Time to go to plan B, I called my son-in-law, Donnie, who's a certified lifeguard and was as tall as the man who lost the ring. Donnie jumped at the chance, and we met the next afternoon at low tide.

When Donnie and I met the next day, I showed him the area as well as the landmark, and he headed straight out into the ocean. I worked closer to the shore out to about my chest deep. I'm confident we covered the area as completely and thoroughly as we could with nothing to show for it.

In this case, I honestly think he was just out to deep and in an area that made the probability of recovery impossible.

A Little Detective Work

I received a text message at 9:30 in the morning, from a Nashville, Tenn. phone number about a lost ring in the sand. Additional information in the text said that they were leaving to go back home the next day. I immediately called and talked to Ed. He told me that his wife, Diane, had lost her engagement ring in the dry sand the previous day. He was wondering if I could help try to find it. I told him I'd be glad to help. After getting the name of their resort I was on my way and arrived 20 minutes later. This search should be pretty easy, but what concerned me is the ring has been in the dry sand for at least 24 hours. The area they lost it in is hunted pretty regularly and very heavily. I was keeping my fingers crossed.

I met Ed on the beach, and he told me Diane had put her three rings in one of her beach bags. At some point later, their kids had gotten into the bag to get their towels, and other items and her rings ended up in the sand. Ed and their 13-year-old son, Greg, looked through the sand and found two of the rings, one being her wedding band. The one still lost was her beautiful Platinum with Diamonds engagement ring.

Ed pointed out the area, and I started with a north/south grid search with my PI. I searched for an hour and a half where he thought the ring might be and wasn't finding it. I also searched the area Ed, and his son found the other two rings, and I still wasn't having any luck. I tested the Platinum wedding band three different times, the first time in the sand was a good signal, a little while later a second test in the sand was a sporadic signal and the third test was with the wedding band on Ed's finger, and I got nothing! It concerned me

119

enough that I went back home and got my Garrett AT Pro and went back and searched the same area – still no engagement ring. By now it'd been a 3-hour search, and I was baking in the heat and was getting tired, so I called my friend, Jim Brouwer. I asked him if he was available to help. Jim has never hesitated to come running if he could, so he said he'd be there in 30 minutes. I was starting to wonder if my intuition about someone finding it was right.

Meanwhile, I went back to Ed and Diane asking questions, hoping to get a new clue about where the ring might be. After a short period, Greg spoke up and said a couple of things about where he thought it might be. I asked Greg to come with me and tell and show me what he remembered. He had a somewhat different version, and he had me a little farther north and closer to the high tide line. Greg also mentioned that they had been digging a hole in the sand the day before and he was pretty sure we were right next to that same hole. Right before I started searching the new area, Ed said he and Diane were going to take the kids up to the hotel to get some lunch. It's a good feeling to know you project trust and honesty where people feel comfortable enough to leave you alone searching for their thousand dollars plus ring!

I started a new, smaller grid search in the area Greg showed me. About 10 minutes into an expanded search, I had to move a couple of beach chairs and umbrellas. What a difference that made. About 10 seconds after moving everything, I hit a target showing a 46 on the screen of the AT Pro. The 46 is the same number that Diane's wedding band had when I tested it. I dug a shallow scoop of sand, dumped in on the beach and saw Diane's beautiful ring looking up at me. I called Jim to tell him he didn't need to come but too late, he had just pulled in the parking lot.

Next, I text Ed, and all I said was "BINGO" and added a picture of Diane's engagement ring. Meanwhile, Jim had walked out on the beach and met me. We were discussing the ring find when I saw Ed running out on the beach. He had gotten my text but hadn't gotten the picture until he was about halfway out on the beach. He had told Diane that I was trying to text him and left her and the kids sitting at the table. He couldn't believe I found the ring.

Ed and I walked back up to where Diane was, and I told him I was going to play with her a little bit. We got to the table, and I looked at Diane and said how hot and tired I was and she was sympathetic, and then I hit her with "but I found it." To say she was overjoyed would be an understatement!!! She jumped up from her chair and came flying around the table to give me a huge hug. I knew she and Ed were very grateful and happy she had her ring back. Their trip back home the next day will be a more relaxed trip, I'm sure. I gave a big thank you to Greg, who was a tremendous help and saved me a few extra hours of searching.

I received the following from Ed and Diane on my post.

We are SO thankful to Jim. His hard work and dedication really made the difference in finding this ring. After the first hour, we thought it was basically hopeless. Jim kept pushing on, trying a different detector, trying different areas and talking to everyone he could to get a better idea of where the ring might be. He was not going to give up — and he didn't! Strangers on the beach were still cheering and talking about him long after he found our ring.

The ring was insured, but no amount of insurance money would have given us back what Jim gave us — the original ring with all its associated sentimental value. Jim, you are a wonderful man, and you turned a potentially very sad situation into a joyous memory we will cherish. Thank you so much!!

Ed & Diane.

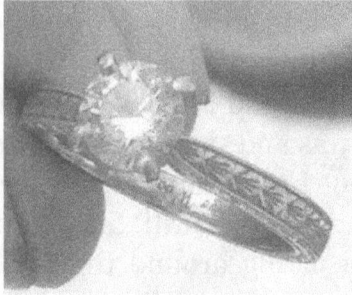

Playing with his Kids

Eleazar called me a little before 7 a.m. on Friday, August 12th asking if I could help find his Platinum wedding band that he lost the day before. He said he was in knee to waist deep water right around mid-tide. Unfortunately, Jim Brouwer and I were on our way to North Carolina to look for another lost ring from 6 days earlier. I told Eleazar that I would call him back when we finished that search and set up a time to meet. Jim and I finished up the first search with negative results, so we headed back to North Myrtle Beach. I called Eleazar and told him we would meet him on the beach in about an hour and a half.

Eleazar met Jim and me as we pulled into a parking spot and took us to the area that he, his wife, Natalie, and two children had been sitting the day before. Eleazar told us he didn't sleep at all the night before. He got to the beach early so he could lay claim to the same spot they were at yesterday when he lost his ring. He had chairs set up, towels laying around, and I think, some of the kid's toys to ensure nobody could get close to "his" spot.

He explained that he had been playing with the kids and boogie boarding about the mid-tide line. Shortly after being in the water is when he realized his ring had come off. He had made numerous observations on landmarks around his location when he lost his ring.

Jim took the water line and worked the incoming tide while I took the dry sand and worked my way down to the mid-tide line. I wanted to rule out the possibility that he lost his ring in or around the area where they were sitting before the crowds started showing up. Neither Jim nor I were getting many targets, and we were both confident that we had completely covered the area from the dry sand to the mid tide line. There was a lot of sand on the beach, but the ring should still be accessible after just a day.

Jim and I talked to Eleazar telling him that there wasn't much more we could do at the time. The tide had come back in, making our search that much harder. I told him I'd be back later that evening, and Jim might join me, but I wasn't sure.

I showed back up that evening about 8:30 p.m. which was an hour and twenty minutes before low tide. I started following the tide out in the area that Eleazar showed us earlier, not finding anything at all. I kept working the area and twenty minutes or so before low tide, right around 9:45 p.m., I decided to expand my grid search and moved a little farther south and went into the surf about knee deep. Within twenty to thirty steps I got a loud tone on my new Gold Quest PI. I dug a scoop of sand, washed the sand out in the surf, and heard the heavy Platinum ring rattling around in the scoop. I turned my headlamp on to confirm it and there it was, bright and shiny in the bottom of the scoop. It's such a rush when you find somebody's ring.

I wasn't sure if Jim was on his way to join me, so I called him real quick to let him know I had found it. Luckily, I caught him before he got too far away from home.

I walked back up to the hotel where I had some lights and took a picture of Eleazar's beautiful platinum ring and sent it to him with a text saying "Surprise!!" I immediately got a text back from him saying "I'm on my way." He showed up within seconds with his wife and two kids; it looked like they just got woke up. His excitement was priceless. He was confident his ring was gone forever, and I had started to have my doubts as well. Trying to do a grid search in pitch black conditions, knee deep with a medium surf is tough and scary in itself. I also had to contend with an abundance of jellyfish, which is not a good situation to search for anything, let alone a small ring. But his ring is back on his finger where it belongs.

The next day I got the following comments from Eleazar and Natalie on my blog at The Ring Finders website.

From Eleazar

Here is my story: Immediately after I noticed that my ring was lost I was extremely depressed it was definitely a stomach-churning vacation mood killer. That night I was so upset I couldn't sleep, I was on the internet looking for the same exact ring to replace the one I just lost, but I knew even though it would look the same that it would not feel the same. So I started doing internet searches for metal detectors and advice on how to find a ring in the ocean which thankfully brought me to theringfinders.com and connected me to the North Myrtle beach representative Jim Wren. After reading some of the blogs I had decided to contact Jim as a last hail marry however it was 3 a.m., so I waited until daylight. 6 a.m. comes, and I am antsy not 100% sure which part of the beach/ocean I lost my ring, I took the elevator down to the beach to claim the same area that I was sitting at the day before just in case the ring fell off in that area. Thinking back, it was pretty comical because I set up two beach umbrellas and a few chairs in the RAIN trying to claim the largest area possible before anyone beat me to it. Then a little before 7 a.m. against all my will afraid that I would be waking Jim up I called, he answers, and I nervously ask for help. He says that he was already on a recovery job and would meet me after he finishes. True to his word Jim called me back and asked me to meet him on the beach, he brought Jim Brouwer to assist. The two gentlemen combed the beach and water with no luck. At this point, I have started to accept that my ring would be lost for good and offered to pay Jim for coming out. Totally dedicated to finding my ring, both Jims would not accept any money, and Jim Wren says he wants to come back during low tide which happened to be at 9:51 p.m. So the remainder of the day becomes a waiting game moping around with high anxiety. Then at approximately 9:50 p.m. I get a text from Jim Wren "SURPRISE" with pictures of my ring in complete disbelief and heightened excitement I jump up and down screaming "Holy $#!* He found my ring!!!!!"

I do not regret losing my ring because I got the pleasure of meeting two genuinely kind men with extremely large hearts. My only regret was not calling Jim sooner; I may have saved a sleepless night.

Thank you so much for taking your time to recover my ring. My whole family appreciates all your efforts.

From Natalie
To think you can actually recover a lost ring in the ocean. I was reluctant when Eleazar called Jim for help. Jim was true to every word he said to us. He

showed up when he said he would and found Eleazar's ring in that choppy ocean. Jim was in knee deep water with jellyfish trying to find something that wasn't his and not expecting a dime if he found anything. Jim is an amazing person! I am still in shock that he was able to recover my husband's wedding band! Thank you, Jim! I would recommend Jim for the job without hesitation. What he did for us and what he can do for others is wonderful! Call him as soon as you lose something on the beach. He will be there within the hour if he's not on a job. He's so nice, knows what he's doing, and will keep searching to find your treasure. What a guy!

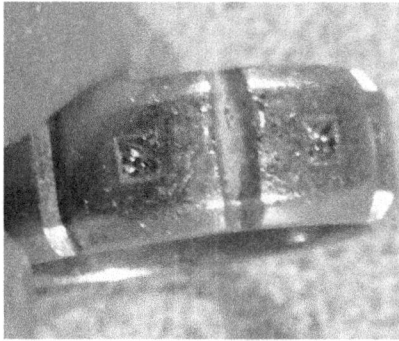

Disappeared in the Surf

I was out one beautiful afternoon metal detecting a particular spot I like to hit. A lady came up to me asking if I'd found a platinum wedding band. I hadn't, so I started inquiring as to what the circumstances were with the loss. She told me her son had lost his ring a couple of days before, around the area I was searching. I asked if I could talk to him so I could find out if he wanted me to help and could give me a better description of the area and the ring. She called him, and he met me shortly after.

When we met, I told him I was a member of The Ring Finders, gave him my card and showed him the website on my iPhone. He said he'd like for me to try and find it and that his wedding band was a size 13 platinum ring. He showed me the area he lost it in which was a lot further out than his mother thought. He explained that it came off when he was sitting in the surf and had his hands down in the sand just enjoying the moment. When he pulled his hands out of the sand, his ring was gone. The area he was talking about was still pretty deep, so I told him I could be back in a few hours when the tide was going out. We agreed to meet at the area at 6 p.m.

I showed up at 6, and he was waiting for me. We walked out in the area he lost it, and it was still underwater and wasn't going to be any shallower at low tide. He was a big guy, so him sitting in the water would still be at least knee deep. I wasn't very optimistic about finding it for a few reasons. With the weight and size of his ring, it was going to sink quickly. It had also been under water and in the sand for at least 48 hours, which meant the currents and surf were continually pushing more sand on top of it. Finally, I don't think he knew exactly where he lost his ring.

I made my way into the surf, which was a little rough, and he was right behind me. He had me detect over different spots that he thought he lost it. I had no luck that night nor the two to three other times I went back to search. My thought is his ring is buried so deep in the sand a detector isn't going to pick it up. Maybe someone will find it one of these days when a big storm moves a lot of sand out to sea.

Back Together

I originally received a phone call on August 11th from Jeff stating he had lost his wedding band in the ocean. He went on to say he had been in and out of the water over the course of a few hours and wasn't sure when, where or how deep he was when it slipped off his finger. I knew right off the bat that this was going to be a hard search. I knew the resort he was at, and it's a pretty good size in comparison to some of the others around the area. Plus not knowing any details of where exactly he lost it, made this a vast search area.

I was just wrapping up another ring find, with Jim Brouwer's help, and was waiting for the couple to come back to the beach to get their ring when Jeff called. Jim agreed to go ahead and head to Jeff's resort and start looking. As soon I made the ring return from the search I was on, I headed up the road to catch up with Jim.

When I got to the resort Jeff had stayed at, Jim already had a grid search going from the mid tide line seaward. I started a grid search a little further down the beach and worked seaward to about thigh to waist deep. After a few hours, the tide turned, and we weren't having any luck. It was getting dark, and neither one of us had our headlamps, so we called it quits. I made at least three maybe four more trips out and searched north/south and east/west grids and felt confident that I had covered the area as well as I could. Because of the size of the resort, I know the beach behind it is heavily detected. Although I wasn't planning on giving up altogether, I thought this would be a ring that I just couldn't find.

Fast forward to Oct 8th when Hurricane Mathew passed just offshore east of Myrtle Beach as a Cat 1 hurricane. There wasn't near the sand movement on the beach that we (the guys that metal detect) had hoped for, but we did get some. I had three lost rings that I had gotten calls on that summer that I wasn't able to find. I thought maybe this would be an excellent opportunity to give each one another shot. Jeff's ring was number 2 on my list, so I had planned on going out over the next few days for one last crack at it. Oddly enough, Jeff text me Saturday evening (Oct 15th) asking: "did the hurricane wash up my ring?" We text back and forth, and I let him know I was planning to go out and give it one more shot.

Shortly after we finished texting, I contacted my son-in-law, Donnie, and asked if he was available to help try and find this ring sometime the coming week. We set it up to search at low tide Monday (Oct 17th).

That Monday, I got there maybe 10 minutes before Donnie and was working a grid from the middle of the resort north. My grid search was from the wet sand to about chest deep in the ocean. When Donnie showed up, I had him start his grid from the south end of the resort and work north to the middle of the resort. By both of us working on a northerly search, we could cover the entire area without our machines interfering with each other. We could also cover the area in half the time and before the tide turned.

I was digging a target in the wet sand about 10 minutes after Donnie had started his grid search. I was trying to get my target out of the sand when he walked up behind me and dropped a ring in the sand at my feet. I looked at it and thought it might be Jeff's ring but wasn't positive. Jeff had told me what the inscription on the inside of the ring said, so at least I had a reference. We confirmed the inscription on the inside of the ring with what Jeff had told me and damn if we didn't have a match! I was shocked that we recovered the ring from the ocean two months after being lost. Donnie did a great job and really helped me out with this one! I sure appreciated his help.

I took a picture of the ring and sent it by text to Jeff and then I called him. In his own words, he was speechless. I'll never know whether the hurricane helped move enough sand or the spring tide (lower than average tides) helped us get out to a deeper part of the ocean. Nonetheless, Jeff had his ring back where it belonged. Along with the picture he sent me of him and his wife, Michelle, he also sent me a picture with their hands together titled "Back Together." There's nothing more I can add!

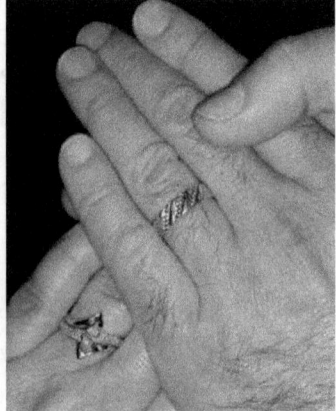

5 "Golden" Rings!!

On Friday, June 17th, I got an e-mail from Josh that said, in part, that he lost five rings in the ocean and wondered if there was any way I could help. We went back and forth via email, and I finally asked for his cell number so I could call and get the details. As I was calling him, I'm thinking – 5 rings, must have had them on a towel and flipped the towel or something along those lines. I was also thinking, is this for real?

When he answered his phone the first question I asked was: "is this legit?" He assured me it was and said that he was wearing all five rings and throwing a football back and forth with a friend in the surf, probably not a good thing. He went on to say his ring finger that he was wearing his class ring on, swelled up, so he moved the ring to his pinky finger. A few catches later, and the football knocks the ring into the surf. At that point, Josh said he took the other four rings off and put them on a chain he had around his neck. Guess where the football hit next, yep, broke the chain and all four rings hit the water and disappeared. He was able to save his gold chain though!

He told me he was back home in Virginia and that this had happened the previous Saturday. He gave me the hotel name and a good idea of the location and said he lost them in knee-deep water about 1 p.m. Looking at the tide tables for that day I saw that high tide was within an hour of him losing the rings. No problem, the rings should be pretty close to the high tide line. On my way to the beach, he sends me a text saying he remembered that he and his buddies all got up early that morning for breakfast. He said in the text that they were on the beach and he lost the rings about

10 a.m. Ok, now my search was going to be farther down the beach and in the surf. This time change could make this find a little tougher depending on the waves and wind. Plus, after a week with them all being gold, they could be buried deep in the sand or someone could have found them by now.

When I got there, I scoped out the area and realized with me having a bad ankle, the size of the area to search, and fighting an incoming tide that I could use some help. I called my friend, Jim to see what he was doing. At the time, he said he was busy and wouldn't be able to make it. About 5 minutes later he called me back saying he needed a break and would be right there.

I had already started a north/south grid working parallel to the surf line when he showed up. I drew a line in the sand down the middle of the search area and Jim worked the north side, and I worked the south.

At some point, I decided I'd start going perpendicular to the ocean doing an east/west grid line. I went from about waist deep in the water to close to the high tide line. The fourth line I got a loud tone and dug out two rings (one stuck inside the other). WHAM!! I had found the right spot just above the mid-tide line. I got Jim's attention, and he came up to help find the other three rings. Again, I started with a north/south grid starting at my mid-point line I had made. Jim made a couple of passes around the spot and found two more of the rings. About 10 minutes later, Jim hit the 5th ring, which was the class ring. It was about nine feet away from the spot of the other four. I sent Josh a picture of me wearing all five rings, and he responded with "OMG!"

I got Josh's address and wrapped up the rings and sent them home. I got a text from Josh a few days later that he finally got his rings back. He was very grateful!

I received the following response on my blog from Josh.

Thank you so much. I never thought there was even a chance to ever see one of them again.

A Saved Vacation

I got a call from Matt at 7 a.m., asking if I could help try and find his wife, Denise's, wedding and engagement ring set. He said that she lost it in the afternoon, the day before, in waist deep water. I got the location and told him I'd call him when I got there. It took me a little while to wake up and get ready. When I finally got going, I grabbed my gear and headed towards the beach. On the drive, I could tell it was going to be one of those nasty days with a lot of rain. I was just hoping there'd be no lightning.

I got there about an hour later, called Matt, and met him on the beach. By now, it was starting to rain pretty heavily. Matt showed me the area where Denise was when she lost her ring and gave me the description. The time that Matt gave me when she lost the rings would have put it right on the high tide line. So, if she was waist deep, then the ring should be around the mid-tide area. I started my grid search parallel to the water and was about ankle deep. I wanted to get this area searched before the tide started coming back in. After doing a grid search for 30 minutes, I was confident the ring wasn't in the lower section of the beach. I moved up the beach and started a new grid just above the mid-tide line working back towards the surf. All of sudden the sky opened up, and I was getting drenched.

About 30 minutes into my second grid search, I got a tone and the only one I'd had that morning. I dug a scoop of wet sand and dumped it on the beach. I ran my coil over the hole and then over the scoop of sand. The target was out of the hole, but I couldn't see anything. I spread the sand out with my foot and there it was – KA-Boom!!! What a beautiful ring. I cleaned the ring off and sent Matt a picture and a text saying, "Found it!" I told Matt I'd meet him inside the hotel so he wouldn't have to get wet. As I'm heading off the beach, I hear thunder off in the distance, so I'm glad I finished this one. I met Matt inside the hotel, and he said Denise was coming down from the room.

As Denise came out of the elevator I could tell she had been crying; I'm sure it was because I found her treasure and they were tears of joy. Her expression when I handed it back to her said it all, and she stated: "I thought I'd never see it again." Thankfully, not only did she get to see it again, but she got to put it back on her finger where it belonged. Big handshake from Matt and a distant hug from Denise, distant because I was soaked and didn't want to get her wet. Another great vacation with a happy ending and additional memories.

Matt posted the following on my blog.

We are very grateful for what you've given back to us. Thanks again for saving our trip!"

Craigslist Posting

I saw and responded to a posting on Craigslist about a Man's lost wedding band. The post showed a picture and described the ring as a Tungsten ring lost at Sunset Beach, N.C. Not hearing anything back on my email and having some spare time I decided to go ahead and conduct a couple of searches. I didn't have a whole lot of information to go on but enough to at least try. I was hoping I'd find the ring and be able to return it. After a couple of trips, I didn't have any luck finding anything.

Two days later, I received an email from Aimee saying her and her husband Steven would love my help. After exchanging a few emails, she told me that Steven had been skimboarding in a two-block area. This area was much larger than described in the Craigslist posting. There was no way I could cover that big of an area by myself. I knew I'd need some help.

I contacted my son-in-law, Donnie, who had helped me on a few other searches. I told him what the situation was and asked him if he wanted to help me. I said we'd have to go at low tide which was fine with him because he didn't have to work the next day. About 3 hours later we were on the beach to catch the 2 a.m. low tide. Normally, I don't go out at this time of night just for safety reasons, but I felt very safe going to Sunset Beach.

Looking over the area to search, I sent Donnie south to cover one block while I headed north to cover the second block. Because we had a full moon, the spring tide was super low, providing us more beach for searching. After a little more than 2 hours of searching, Donnie started waving his flashlight to get my attention. I walked the block to catch up to him, and I asked him if he'd found it. His response was: "I think so" and handed me the ring. I broke out my phone and checked the picture on the Craigslist posting. Shockingly, we had a match between the ring in hand and the photo of the ring in the post. I was very pleasantly surprised we found the ring; I honestly thought that with the size of the area and the time the ring was in the sand, it was going to be impossible to find it. I think it was close to 5 a.m. by the time we got home.

I contacted Aimee later that morning and told her the good news. She was shocked and couldn't have been more excited. Neither one of them could believe we found the ring after being lost in the sand for five days.

Luckily they were still in the area, so I delivered the ring to them. Handshakes and hugs all around.

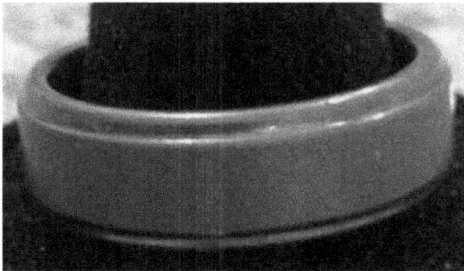

Heart Grabbers

Every lost ring call I get is very significant and unique in one way or another. Once in a while, I get a call that just pulls at my heartstrings a little more than usual. I can't explain why maybe it's being told the whole story that goes with the ring. These stories without a doubt got to me.

Three Month Search

I had initially received an email from Katy on Sept 23rd telling me her husband had lost his tungsten wedding band while body surfing on Sept 15th. The email also said they had been on a family vacation at Ocean Isle Beach, N.C. when the incident happened. We exchanged quite a few emails back and forth, including the circumstances and location of the loss. Katy sent one email saying that: "she doesn't share this story with very many people" and enclosed a picture with the story. After I read the couple's story and saw the picture, my heart melted, and I was determined I would give it my all to find this ring. Their story is personal and private, and it's not my place to share it.

One of the other things Katy had told me in one of her emails is that her husband had lost his ring at 4 p.m. I checked the tide tables for the day he lost it and discovered he lost it right at high tide. Running all the details through my mind, I was confident the ring should be between the mid and low tide lines. I checked the tide table for the next low tide and was on my way.

I got to the beach and conditions were horrible, the waves were big and crashed on the beach. I waded out and was getting hammered by the waves when I got a good signal (which was not the ring). In the process of trying to dig the target, I literally got picked up by a wave and thrown down in the water. In an unsuccessful attempt to try and catch myself, I ended up breaking the arm cuff attached to the shaft of my detector. Anybody that metal detects knows how difficult it can be in rough seas, or any seas for that matter without an arm cuff. So basically I was without a machine for the surf and called my son-in-law, Donnie. I told him what was going on and what I was looking for and asked him if he could help. When he showed up, he did the surf, getting knocked around and I did the wet sand. We searched for about three hours, and neither one of us had much luck. The targets we did find were almost unreachable with our detectors because of all the sand on the beach. Nothing looked promising at all.

A few days later, still without an arm cuff for my machine, I borrowed a detector from Matt Fry, a member of The Ring Finders in Myrtle Beach to give it another shot. When I got to the beach, the conditions were worse than the first try with even more sand. There was a mound of sand between the mid and low tide line all the way down the beach. Again I waded out in the waves, getting pounded as I went. In the process of searching, I got lifted up by a wave and slammed down. This time I tried to brace myself, buried Matt's coil into the sand and broke the shaft. Ok, this was not turning out to be an easy recovery. I got my White's PI, and the shaft of Matt's machine fixed and was ready to go with my PI.

Meanwhile, we had been getting some big hurricanes and storms off the coast that were driving tons of sand up on the beach. From the details I got from Katy on where her husband lost his ring, I was confident the ring was there but getting buried deeper by all the sand. I was bound and determined I was going to find this ring, so I kept going back hoping for better conditions and less sand.

After at least seven trips by me and a couple from Donnie, I felt the ring was slipping away. On Dec 18th, when I got to the beach at low tide I couldn't believe what I was seeing. Calmer seas (at least for this shoreline), at least a foot to a foot and a half of sand off the beach, and a big cut in the sand on the upper beach. I started a north/south grid search from low tide out to about thigh deep; the water was really getting cold!!!! Thigh deep was my limit. I worked my way up the beach, going from the low tide line to the high tide line and started an east/west grid. Probably about my seventh grid line, I got a so-so hit on my PI that I dug. The target was down a good 12-15 inches. I finally got it out of the hole and dumped the scoop of sand on the beach. When I saw the clump of sand around the object, I thought I had a bottle cap. I picked the target up with the scoop, shook the scoop to separate the sand and bingo there was the lost ring. I knew in an instant; I had the right one. I just stood there in awe, three months and three days, 8th trip and I had it. Even I couldn't comprehend this one, after all this time I had it.

I flew home to check the picture Katy had sent me. I had her husband's ring in my hand. I called her, reintroduced myself and said "I've got two questions.

First, what is your husband's name and secondly what's the address to mail his ring back to him." She just couldn't believe it, and with every question she asked, her voice cracked a little more until she just lost it, which made me lose it until neither one of us could talk. I text her a quick picture, and I heard her say "he found it." Then we had a true serendipity moment, she and her family were just finishing up with an early Christmas, opening presents, etc. when I called. She put me on speaker phone, and I think everyone there was in shock. She also informed me a little later that on Dec 28th her and Will, her husband, will be celebrating their 4th Wedding Anniversary. The timing was perfect; finding their ring, calling at the moment I did, and getting their ring back to them before both Christmas and their Anniversary.

Man's Gold and Diamond Ring

I got a call from Kelly after he found me through The Ring Finders website asking if I could help find his ring that was extremely sentimental to him. He described the ring as a 14k yellow gold ring with a 2ct diamond center stone, which came from his mother's wedding ring set. He also said there were an additional 50 diamonds that ran down both sides of the ring with yellow gold strips on each side of the ring, as well. Kelly said this ring, "was specially designed and made" for him by his friend Manny Sharp of Sharp Jewels in N.Y. and he desperately wanted to get it back. To him the ring was priceless.

He told me that he had taken his ring off at the beach and placed it in his ball cap and laid it on the wet sand. After throwing a ball around with his friends, he grabbed his hat off the beach and put it on forgetting about the ring. He realized it a few minutes later, but the ring had already fallen out of the hat and buried itself in the sand.

My wife and I had been on a little mini vacation and on our way home when he called. We were still about 2 hours away, so I wasn't able to get to the beach for a few hours.

When I finally arrived at the hotel parking lot, I called him and headed for the beach. Within minutes he came out of the hotel onto the beach. He showed me an area about 30 X 20 yards to search that was closer to the high tide line. It was now almost low tide, so I had plenty of search time. I added my additional 10-15 yards on all sides of his search area, so I didn't have to go back and research if the ring wasn't inside his suspected area. After about 40 minutes and eight passes in the grid, and a few feet outside of Kelly's area – Cha-Ching!! I got a loud tone on my PI and dug up a scoop of sand, lightly shook out the sand and WOW. I saw this fantastic ring staring up at me from the bottom of the scoop.

I walked back over to where Kelly was sitting Indian style on the beach and asked him to explain the details to me one more time. I think he was getting a little irritated with me because I kept asking questions as I searched just to make sure I was on track. Kelly started giving me the details and describing his ring again while looking towards the area he lost it. Before he turned his head back towards me, I held his ring up so he'd see it. When he turned his head and saw his ring - BAM! I don't think I have ever seen somebody move so quickly from a sitting to a standing position. A few beachgoers were sitting around watching and broke out in applause and congratulations. I got some sincere hugs and thank yous from Kelly.

Lost Birthday Present

On Sunday, July 16th, I got a heartfelt email from Sarah wondering if I had found a man's 14K wedding band in the Cherry Grove area of North Myrtle Beach S.C. Her email said her husband had lost his the previous Thursday night, July 13th. I wrote back that I hadn't and asked her for some details, the time it was lost and where her husband Eric was on the beach (dry or wet sand or in the water). We went back and forth with numerous emails including some google satellite maps with areas of the beach highlighted.

Every ring call is extraordinary in its own way, but occasionally you get one that just tugs at your heart for whatever reason. When she wrote saying that her husband's original ring was getting too big for him, she had bought him this new one and gave it to him on his birthday last month; she had me. We ended our emails with me telling her that "I can't promise miracles but I do promise you I'll give it my best shot."

A few hours later I was on the beach working from the dry sand to the mid-tide area that she highlighted on the google map going outside the area on all four sides. After a little over 3 hours and finding very little I called it a night, knowing I was going back out first chance I had. I sent Sarah an email saying I hadn't had any luck. I did not let her know I was planning on going back out.

Monday morning I got an email from her thanking me for looking and offering a gratuity for time and gas. I wrote back telling her thanks, but it was my pleasure, and that I was planning on going back out, I didn't want her thinking I had given up.

Tuesday morning, I woke up early so I could be out on the beach working the outgoing tide to the low tide line. Another 3 hours plus and again I'm not finding very much of anything after going from thigh deep at low tide to the high tide line doing both north/south and east/west grids.

By now I've got about 40 yards of upper beach left to search, the crowds are starting to show up, taking some of my search area away and I really had no place else to search. BANG, I got a booming signal on my Gold Quest SS PI. Dug a scoop and flipped it out on the sand and there it was, I was 99% sure I had the right ring.

Sarah had told me about the very special inscription she had put on the inside of the ring, but I didn't have my glasses, and there was no way I could read what it said. I walked down the beach to a small pool of water and washed the ring off. I then walked up to a much younger man playing with his son and asked him if he could tell me what the inscription said giving him the first two words, he read the rest, and I had it.

I played it over in my head on how I was going to tell Sarah I found it. So, I sent her an email saying my email was acting up and if she would please call me or give me a number to call her because I had a couple more questions.

When she called, I gave her a little pity story about how I'd been searching, blah, blah, blah and then I said I've got a couple of questions to ask 1-what's your husband's name and 2-what address do I send his ring back to? She caught on instantly and said "you found it?", and tears of joy flowed.

I put it in the mail the same day, and it was on its way home!! A little later in the afternoon, she sent me the following text that put a smile on my face – "And you said you couldn't promise a miracle!"

I got another text message a few days later from Sarah that she had received the ring and giving me another big Thank you. Mission Accomplished!!!

I received the following in my post from Sarah.

I am still in total shock that this amazing man found my husband's ring! When we got home from vacation, I thought to check if maybe somebody had found the ring and posted it online. Knowing this was extremely unlikely and having complete doubt that this had actually happened, I saw no harm in searching anyway. So I searched "ring found Cherry Grove, N Myrtle Beach." And the Ring Finders page resulted in my search. I clicked on it because it sounded interesting. I couldn't believe these awesome people even exist as I read through the webpage. So I gave it a whirl, searched the area where our ring was lost, and Jim's name popped up. Well, he told you the rest of the story from there.

However, what he didn't tell you, is that he is a hero and the most selfless person on earth. He spent hours of his time, going out 2 separate times to check all tide levels for me, a total stranger. And not expecting anything in return from me! He never once said "I charge X amount" or asked if I would be paying him for his time. He even spent $8 to ship it to me!

I love to tell this story, and everyone I share it with loves to hear it. All smiles and awe. Not only for the fact that Jim found the ring, but also for the unexpected kindness of this man.

Jim- You have amazed me... Thank you for being you and for finding our lost treasure! I hope you win the lottery or something... you deserve so much and more... you're the man!

Stephen F. Austin State University Ring

On Friday, September 11th, 2015 I got a call from Evan. He asked if I could look for his ring he lost on August 7th, while on vacation in North Myrtle Beach from Little Elm, Texas. When he called, I was on a little weekend vacation with my wife, and at the time we were on a tour boat in Charleston, S.C. going over to Ft. Sumter. I told him I'd be glad to look, and I'd call him back on Sunday when I got home for the details.

I couldn't wait until Sunday, so I ended up texting and then calling Evan Saturday night. He provided a general vicinity of where he lost his ring but nothing definitive. In our initial conversation, he said he was not familiar with North Myrtle Beach and was uncertain of the name of the beach where his ring vanished. Evan told me that he was on vacation with his wife, Summer, and visiting with his friend from law school, Gary, and his family. Evan and Gary attended law school together in Oklahoma from 2002 to 2005, and in their downtime found adventures traveling, watching ball games and getting into the usual mischief that college students are famous for. The two have continued to stay in touch since school, and often take turns visiting with one another in Texas and the Carolinas. Evan told me he recalled Gary saying they were close to Cherry Grove beach when the ring was lost.

During one of our many phone conversations, Evan confided in me that he has cerebral palsy and confined to an electric wheelchair. The ring he lost was his College Ring and was extremely sentimental to him. I could easily deduce from our conversations that this ring was a symbol of his independence, and a display of his driven spirit to complete his undergraduate degree on his own away from home in Nacogdoches, Texas. This accomplishment in his life meant so much to him, and it was a symbol and constant reminder of that beginning in his life.

Evan sent me a video that Summer filmed on August 7th, showing Gary carrying Evan out into the surf. Gary, knowing Evan's desire for thrills and adventure (some of which have included skydiving, water skiing, snow sledding and four wheeling in the mud), wanted Evan to say he had been in the Atlantic. Gary physically carried Evan in his arms to about waist deep water, and there were sounds of the longtime friends amusingly chuckling as to weight gain and getting old. At some point, they were both knocked over by a wave, which caused Evan's ring to fly off his finger and disappear into the surf. Fortunately, the video showed Gary carrying Evan past 2 posts stuck in the sand with a sign attached to one of the posts indicating a drainage pipe. This video narrowed the search area substantially, but I still wasn't positive on their exact location.

Early Sunday evening, I went to the presumed area looking for the 2 posts with a sign and the drainage pipe. There were two possible locations about three blocks apart. I did a 360-degree video of both locations and sent them back to Evan and Summer to look over and see if anything looked familiar. He and his wife both were pretty sure the 1st video was the right spot. I returned later that evening and searched until just above low tide at 2:30 a.m.

I went back again on Monday at low tide, and I still wasn't convinced I was in the right spot. Evan was finally able to get a hold of Gary and Gary's father on Wednesday and confirmed I was in the right area. Found out later, Gary's father is a neighbor of mine that lives about eight houses down on my street. Evan, Gary and their wives actually stayed just down the street from me while on vacation in August of 2015. Unfortunately, Evan didn't know The Ring Finders existed until he got home and searched the internet a month later.

Thursday I was back at the same spot and searched from the dry to the wet sand and out into knee deep surf. Still no luck except for totally cleaning the dry sand of every bottle cap, pull tabs and other pieces of trash in a 25 X 75-yard area!!! Meanwhile, I was emailing back and forth with friend Jim Brouwer, president of one of the metal detecting hunting clubs in Myrtle Beach, to see if he knew of anybody in the club that might have found the ring. In one of the emails, Jim asked me if I had found the ring yet, and I told him, "no, but was going back out on Saturday at 4 p.m. (outgoing tide) and if he wanted to come out, to come on".

Saturday, I got there a little early after studying the video Evan had sent me over and over again. I tried to position myself exactly where I thought Gary had started walking on the way out into the surf. Then, I estimated the angle that Gary walked since he didn't walk straight in. I counted the number of steps (38) by Gary before the wave knocked him and Evan down, and estimated the length of each step that Gary took. I drew out a square gridline dragging my scoop in the sand leaving a dig line. I drug my scoop at the angle I thought Gary walked from the spot he began to the low tide line, and then started my grid search. Jim showed up around 5 and started another grid to the south of where I was. My search was from North to South, and Jim's was from South to North. After a number of passes, I had to stop because Jim's detector was interfering with mine. I had the sensitivity turned up as high as possible, so I could get the machine searching as deep in the sand as it could. Jim ended up moving a little further south and started working a North to South grid. Right at 6:15 p.m. I had a medium signal right under the angle line that I had marked in the sand. I kept digging and digging; the target was deep. Finally, I got the target out of the hole, and Holy Moly, I had Evan's College Ring in my scoop. I couldn't believe I found it and I'm positive my eyes watered up.

After six weeks and a day of being lost, I wasn't sure I could find the ring. We've had a lot of sanding over on the beach, and I knew the sand was burying the ring deeper and deeper. Plus, there's always the possibility of another metal detectorist finding it. Like I said earlier, I had my PI set at maximum sensitivity and it took 4 or 5 scoops to pull it out from a depth of at least 10-12 inches or more.

When Evan shared his story with me on just how important his ring was to him it truly touched me, so I couldn't wait to call him and Summer. In the course of just a few days, I had called Evan so many times, asking question after question about the ring. The last time I had called him before finding his ring, I apologized for bothering him so much. His response was "Jim; you're not bothering me at all if you have any questions call me!" So, after I found his ring, I called him. I started telling him how many days I've been out there, how bad the conditions were, and how Jim and I had been out that day for about 3 hours. After hearing my pity story, his response was, "Jim, I understand". I know he felt his ring was gone forever. Then I followed with, "Evan, you told me if I had any more questions to call you." He said, "Yea Jim, what is it?" My response, "Where do I mail your ring back to?" That question blew him away. His mother, sister, and wife were there with him, and he turned around and told them, "He found it!" I could hear them all crying!

I received the following in my post from both Evan and Summer:

Jim,

The reality that my ring was found honestly didn't set in until placing it back on my finger, it's so surreal! This ring carried such sentiment and relocating it will permanently hold a special memory for my entire family. Jim's time, patience, skill, and God-given ability were on full display as this was an extremely difficult recovery. We are eager to return to Myrtle Beach and personally express our gratitude to Jim. In the meantime, we will continue to pray for Jim, his family, and many more successful recoveries! Evan

Jim,

I cannot express to you with words how grateful and thankful I am that you found Evan's ring. Though it is just a piece of gold, his ring is priceless, a symbol of hard work and determination that many could never understand. I was devastated more than he was when it slipped off into the water and I prayed daily that it would be found. I am so thankful that God sent us someone like you to do His work. We will forever be indebted to you and will cherish this ring more than ever before. Thank you for your time, compassion, and kindness. I do hope that one day we can repay you! Summer.

Social Media and the Internet

After every search, find, and the return of someone's lost item, I always write a blog. I post those blogs in my section of "The Ring Finders.com" website as well as, my Facebook page, "The Ring Finders of North Myrtle Beach SC". I tag all my blogs so when someone searches the internet about a lost ring or item in and around North Myrtle Beach SC or SE North Carolina, my blogs pop up. For the most part, my blogs are the first or second search suggestions. Almost every member of The Ring Finders directory does the same thing. Why, because there are so many people that aren't aware of the service that The Ring Finders provides. I'd venture to say, during the summer months, there are easily hundreds of rings left behind in the sandy beaches or shallow waters around the world.

When I make a return, I ask the owners if they'd do me a couple of big favors. First, I ask them to please share their story about their return on their Facebook page and other social media. This helps get the word out about this fantastic service. Secondly, I ask them to write a comment or testimonial about their feelings when they lost their item and our experience together on my blog. There is no better review than someone who has had the experience. Both of these things will help the next person who loses something.

The return I did for Tim and Mary in the chapter titled "Craigslist Posting" had some amazing results. Tim told me he had posted his story on "Reddit". Honestly, I didn't have any idea what Reddit was until I asked my wife. After Tim told me about Reddit, I took a few minutes and went to the site to see for myself. I saw that Tim's post had almost 1900 hits with comments. That's 1900 people that now know about The Ring Finders which I thought was incredible. I have my email server connected to my iPhone. That day my email was going crazy from people visiting my blogs and leaving me great comments who had seen the Reddit post.

Tim also emailed me saying that he tried to get on The Ring Finders website and noticed it's very slow and hoped it wasn't his fault. I tried getting on the website and had the same problem. I figured it wasn't anything to worry about and soon forgot it.

The next day I got a phone call from Chris Turner, CEO, and Founder of The Ring Finders. I'm thinking why is Chris calling me? I answered the phone and he starts the conversation with: "Tell me about this ring return you had yesterday". So I tell him the story and then he says: "The Ring Finders website usually has about 500 hits a month, yesterday we had over 44,000 hits and today, so far, we've had over 18,000 hits. That much activity at one time almost shut the site down." I thought, oh crap, I'm in trouble now. On the contrary, Chris couldn't have been happier that so many people had checked out the website. If there's any downside to this, it's that Chris now has to pay an extra amount of money to have a larger bandwidth for situations that may arise in the future.

In addition to all that publicity, I've also been on the local Myrtle Beach news twice and had Tim's story published in the Huffington news.

Chris Turner's vision is to make The Ring Finders a household name and that the members can help as many people as possible.

I Hope This Never Ends

I hope you have enjoyed reading these true and factual stories as much as I've enjoyed being a part of them. I absolutely love helping people find their lost items but just as heartbroken as they are, when I can't find something of sentimental value. I've had men and women cry on my shoulder and I've shed tears with every one of them and not ashamed to say so.

These are approximately three-quarters of my success stories, some of which I had help with from Jim, Matt, or Donnie and I really appreciated their help. The other finds, although very important, didn't have the sentimental or emotional value. Some of those finds included keys, crosses, crucifixes, and cellphones. There have been a few returns that I wasn't involved in, other than getting the initial call because I was out of town and unavailable. Those are the returns that Jim, Matt, and Donnie stepped up to the plate and knocked it out of the park.

Every individual that I helped was absolutely remarkable under the circumstances of the grief, stress, and uncertainty of losing something very near and dear to their hearts. For that, I am truly honored to have met and helped each and every one of you. Thank you for entrusting me to help find your lost treasures.

I hope this journey never ends.

Thank you!

Jim

Contact Information

Jim Wren
TheRingFinders.com
jim.wren@theringfinders.com